HIST

URQUHART CASTLE

AND THE GREAT GLEN

NICK BRIDGLAND

BATSFORD

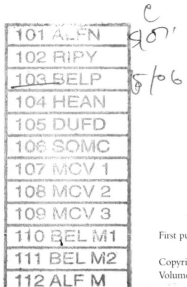
First published 2005

Copyright © Nick Bridgland 2005
Volume © Batsford 2005

The right of Nick Bridgland to be identified as Author of this work has
been asserted by him in accordance with the Copyright, Designs and
Patents Act 1988.

ISBN-13 9780713487480
ISBN-10 0 7134 8748 8

A CIP catalogue record for this book is available from the British Library.

Printed in China by WKT Co. Ltd
for the publishers:

B T Batsford
The Chrysalis Building
Bramley Road
London W10 6SP
www.batsford.com

Distributed in the United States and Canada by Sterling Publishing Co.,
387 Park Avenue South, New York, NY 10016, USA

Contents

Acknowledgements

Every author likes to feel that their work bears the stamp of originality. However there is one man without whose work, this book would have been very different. William Mackay's 1893 account of the history and folklore of the parish of Urquhart and Glenmoriston is both highly readable and full of detail, belying this lawyer's careful attention to documents. However its greatest value comes in that Mackay also recorded the oral history of the parish just as this collective memory began to fragment and become rare. Mackay's work preserved the stories behind the facts of history and is a treasure-house of further material on the history of the people and places of the parish.

While I retain a special gratitude to William Mackay, the living who deserve thanks are far more numerous. I have tried the patience of many colleagues at Historic Scotland but several deserve special mention. Sally Foster has given me much thoughtful and tactful guidance through the active debates which surround the first millennium AD. Chris Tabraham, Peter Yeoman and Allan Rutherford have each humoured me as I have rehearsed my reinterpretation of the development of the buildings at Urquhart.

For unquestioning helpfulness, I must thank Patricia Weekes and the staff at Inverness Museum and Art Gallery and Ewen Fraser on site at Urquhart. David Henrie has remained good-natured and inventive in meeting my unrealistic requests for photography. Special thanks are due to Bryony Coombs who has been relentlessly cheerful and resourceful in co-ordinating the illustrations and their permissions.

All images are Historic Scotland copyright except: **1** courtesy of Colin Baxter; **6** courtesy of the author; **14**, **35** and **38** courtesy of Inverness Museum and Art Gallery; **32** courtesy of the Highland Photographic Archive; **16** and **19** Crown Copyright, courtesy of Inverness Museum and Art Gallery; **42**, **66** and **71** Coull Castle, courtesy of the Royal Commission on the Ancient and Historical Monuments of Scotland; **15**, **27**, **47**, **48**, **49**, **54**, **57** and **65**, courtesy of the Trustees of the National Museums of Scotland; **22**, **29**, **30**, **31**, **45**, **55** and **58** are based on OS data under license 100017509; **28** was drawn by Christina Unwin; **39**, courtesy of the Duke of Roxburghe; **41**, **63** and **70**, crown copyright reproduced courtesy of the Trustees of the National Library of Scotland; **67**, courtesy of the Provost and Fellows of Worcester College, Oxford; **69**, Courtesy of the Scottish National Portrait Gallery.

My most heartfelt gratitude is reserved for David Taylor. If the meals, the housework and the remarkable talent in spotting square barrows were not enough, his support and advice through every stage of writing this book can never be repaid.

1 The Great Glen, looking south-west down Loch Ness

1

Defining the glen, describing the castle

The Great Glen (**2**) is a chasm, a dramatic slice that cuts straight through the Highlands (**1**). In an area characterized by its mountains, the glen runs for nearly 100km (62 miles) from coast to coast while the land barely rises much over 30m (98ft) above sea level. Its presence is inescapable, its topography unavoidable; the great valley, Glen Mór, has imposed itself on every era of human activity. It is the great passageway from the Atlantic to the North Sea, from the farmland of the east to the islands of the west. Its chain of lochs, Loch Lochy, Loch Oich and Loch Ness, and the namesake rivers that drain them, provided a route before roads.

However, the Great Glen is not a place in itself; it is too long, too narrow, too attenuated for the inhabitants at one end to feel much in the way of community with those at the other. In many ways Glen Mór has functioned as two glens back-to-back, with each facing the sea at its mouth. The north-east half looks to the Moray Firth, the fat farm lands of the Black Isle and the Laigh of Moray, contacts along Britain's east coast and across the North Sea. The south-western half looks down Loch Linnhe to the western archipelago and beyond to Ireland. Glen Mór connects east and west but it does not unify them.

The communities of the Great Glen, like people huddled against a mighty wind, have, historically, been found in the nooks, the alcoves off the main south-west to north-east axis created by smaller valleys. It is these branches, Glen Spean, Loch Arkaig, Glengarry, Glenmoriston and Glenurquhart, which provide the havens for settlement. Sheltered in their own glens, these communities have been bounded by their hills, insulated from their neighbours. They are places that outsiders might know of, but would rarely truly know. Only one of these branches, Glen Spean, emerges from the south-west side of the Great Glen providing a passage to the southern Highlands. This side of Glen Mór is not porous; while the glen provides easy passage between east and west, it has been a barrier between north and south that must be negotiated.

Urquhart Castle sits at the mouth of one of the Great Glen's alcoves, jutting out into the deep waters of Loch Ness. It is one of the best known sights in Scotland. People who have never visited it, who know nothing of Scottish history and who have never even heard its name, will still recognize its shattered tower rising above the waters of Loch Ness. Standing sentinel over one of the world's most famous stretches of water, it is an arresting sight. It has been drawn, painted and photographed for centuries, making it instantly recognizable as a symbol of the Scottish Highlands – noble, ancient, rugged and beautiful. Urquhart's fame has grown out of its aesthetic appeal, the drama of its setting on the lochside and its accessibility on one of the main routes in the Highlands, the road linking Inverness and Fort William down the Great

2 *The Great Glen with its principal lochs, towns and tributary glens*

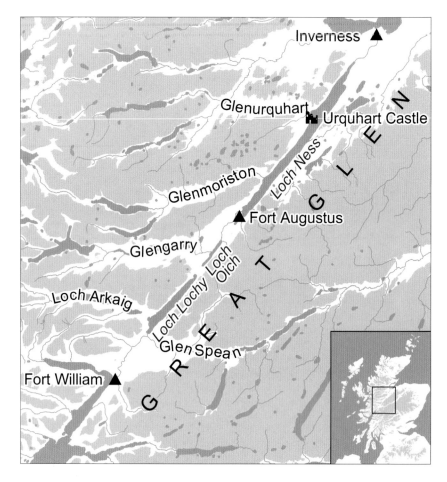

Glen. It has had to cope with the indignity of being the one recognizable feature in countless grainy and modified photographs of its mythical neighbour, the Loch Ness Monster. It is an irony that Urquhart's renown is based almost entirely on its visual appeal, largely ignoring its historical role: a stronghold for over a thousand years, a royal castle, the largest medieval fortress in the Highlands, with associations with St Columba, the Wars of Independence and the lords of the Isles.

A castle in a blind spot

While millions of visitors have walked through the gates of Urquhart Castle (**3**) over the last hundred years, its shattered remains have not received a similar level of

THE LOCH NESS MONSTER

The idea that the waters of Loch Ness hide a mysterious beast is now so well known that it can be surprising to realise how modern this legend is. Highland myths have always been full of tales of spirits and mysterious beasts but as late as the end of the 19th century an account of the folklore of Urquhart and Glenmoriston made no mention of a beast in the loch. In 1933 a report of an large animal rolling and plunging on the surface caught the nation's attention. The arrival of the national press to investigate marked the first summer of Nessie fever. Over the following decades much effort has gone into proving the existence or otherwise of an animal resembling a plesiosaur but consensus has not been reached. What has probably sustained the interest in the Loch Ness Monster for so long is the very lack of certainty; the endless debates between the devotees and sceptics and the sense of mystery imparted to the loch are too enjoyable to give up.

3 *Urquhart Castle on the shore of Loch Ness*

attention from historians, archaeologists or architectural historians. Brief descriptions of the castle appeared at the end of the 19th century in MacGibbon and Ross's *Castellated and Domestic Architecture of Scotland*, and in William Mackay's *Urquhart and Glenmoriston: Olden Times in a Highland Parish* (**4**). However, these were both written before the Ministry of Works transformed the castle between 1913 and 1924 by revealing substantial buildings buried deep beneath the surface (**6**). In 1930 W Douglas Simpson published an article on the castle as revealed by these clearances. Simpson became his generation's foremost expert on Scottish castles, publishing hundreds of articles and books on castles across Britain. He had not been involved in the excavations at Urquhart but he had access to many of the people who were involved, as well as a set of photographs of the site before and during the works. In putting forward his interpretation of the buildings at Urquhart Simpson expressed the difficulties he faced in understanding their development:

> *In attempting to unravel the architectural history of Urquhart Castle, we are confronted, at the outset, by two special difficulties. One is the very uniform character of the rubble masonry throughout the buildings, which makes it exceedingly hard to detect alterations or additions, except where walls come into contact in a way manifestly revealing that one is later than the other … The necessary tamping and pointing operations, which have been carried out with such judicious restraint by H. M. Office of Works, have inevitably contributed to accentuate this difficulty in identifying varieties in texture of masonry … The other difficulty consists in the deplorable extent to which the buildings, with the exception of the Keep, have been robbed of their dressed stones and architectural details which might help to determine dates.*[1]

4 Urquhart Castle before the excavations of the 1920s. Compare with Figure 6

What was true for Simpson at the end of the 1920s remains true today; the masonry at Urquhart is fragmentary and confusing, it lacks much of the carved detail that allows us to put a date to such medieval remains and the conservation works, which were enlightened for the 1920s, have robbed us of much of the subtlety of masonry that can be so helpful in understanding the building. However, while comparatively little new evidence is available to us than was in Simpson's day, the intervening decades have seen great advances in our understanding of Scottish castles in general. While we may be using much the same evidence, we can look at it in a new light.

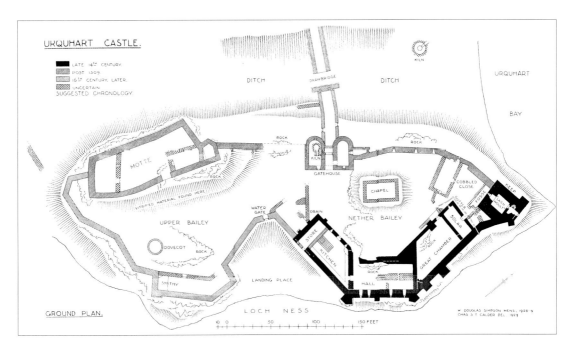

5 *W. D. Simpson's suggested interpretation of the development of Urquhart*

Simpson thought that the earliest part of the surviving structures dated to the late 14th century (**5**). These elements comprised the base of the keep or tower house at the northern tip of the site and the crescent of buildings between the keep and the watergate. He suggested that the walls around the southern edge, the gatehouse and the landward curtain were the work of the early 16th century, while the rest of the curtain wall was constructed a few decades later. He assumed that any earlier structures had been in timber and assigned an uncertain place in the chronology to a considerable number of features. Simpson was aware of the shortcomings of his own work and presented it only as a suggestion. However, the fact that such an authority on Scottish castles had gone to print, identifying the remains at Urquhart as fragmentary and largely late-medieval, meant that Urquhart was subsequently left out of many studies of medieval castle building. Stewart Cruden's *The Scottish Castle*, first published in 1960, almost fails to mention Urquhart altogether, although in many other ways his book is still the most coherent account of the development of military architecture in Scotland over the last thousand years.

The emergence of the masonry castle in Scotland

Cruden set out a pattern for the understanding of Scottish castles from the 11th to the late 13th centuries that has largely withstood half a century of scrutiny. He traced the

6 Urquhart Castle today. Compare with Figure 4

evolution of castle building in Scotland from two sources: timber motte-and-bailey structures (an earthen mound supporting a timber tower with a lower enclosure containing further buildings) had been introduced to England by the Normans and were adopted by the Scottish kings and their adherents as they extended their sphere of control, while the north and west of Scotland, with close cultural ties to Norway and Ireland, had developed a pattern of masonry castle building that seems to have evolved out of earlier patterns of defence – those of using masonry to enhance the natural topography of rocks and headlands. He went on to identify several key stages or branches of development.

Cruden presented Lumphanan, the Doune of Invernochty and, in particular, Rothesay Castle as being good examples of the 'shell keep'; a development of the motte where the summit is no longer simply occupied by a timber tower but rather by a citadel of timber buildings enclosed by a stone perimeter wall. Placing this development in the early 13th century, he suggested that by the late 13th century, castle builders were increasingly abandoning the motte as the location of the highest status accommodation. This shift was influenced by the development in the Holy Land and Edwardian England of the concentric castle, where the defences were arranged as a series of layers and where a masonry curtain wall was enhanced by the construction of towers. Inverlochy, at the south-west end of the Great Glen, is a remarkable example of this new form of castle, with a massive curtain strengthened by large towers (one of which is the donjon tower containing the principal apartments) and entirely encircled by water defences. Cruden saw Bothwell in Lanarkshire and Kildrummy in Mar, with their massive gatehouses, as representing the next logical step in this development. They shared a pattern of design that was characterized by a strong gatehouse, a curtain wall with numerous towers, a massive donjon set to the rear of the site and a substantial stone-built great hall (**7**).

Reassessment of Urquhart

Cruden's work, published 30 years after Simpson wrote his interpretation of Urquhart Castle, presents a model against which the development of Urquhart can be compared and permits the possibility that Simpson greatly underestimated the age of the visible structures. Simpson had the humility to realize that his interpretation of buildings at Urquhart was merely a suggestion, and it is worth emulating that

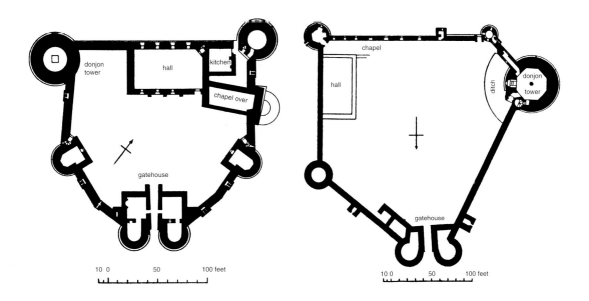

humility here since any reinterpretation of Urquhart's development is unlikely ever to surpass the status of a theory.

Urquhart Castle's long history saw it associated with some of the most powerful figures in medieval Scotland. Although Glenurquhart was never the principal estate of these figures, the scale of the castle and its strategic prominence in the north-east end of the Great Glen gave it a particular importance throughout the Middle Ages. Given this combination of an important site and owners who could marshal vast resources, there are several elements of Simpson's suggestions that might merit questioning. Was it really the case that the best defensive position on the site, the southern summit, only received masonry defences at the start of the 16th century? How likely is it that a medieval castle of this significance had no perimeter walls until the late 16th century, by which time castles on this scale had become an anachronism?

The following reinterpretation of the development of Urquhart is based on a number of separate props: accurate surveying using modern techniques commissioned by Historic Scotland's technical staff has shown slight errors in the information available to Simpson, which may have affected his reasoning; a close reassessment of the details of the buildings has identified features which Simpson may have overlooked; a careful review of the Ministry of Works' papers of the time; a more recent assessment of the artefacts unearthed in the 1920s (information that was not available to Simpson) and the work of those who, over the last three-quarters of a century, have furthered research into the castles of medieval Scotland.

7 *Stewart Cruden's analysis of the original designs of Kildrummy (left) and Bothwell (right) Castles*

Phase 1 – The Pictish fort

The earliest known occupation on the site was identified in limited excavations on the southern summit of the site in the 1980s. It was assumed that what had been found was a defensive core of a larger site, with the lines of its unmortared stone rampart following the shape of the natural rock.

Phase 2 – Possible occupation in the 11th century

The earliest references to a castle at Urquhart suggest that there was something on the site during the period of William the Lion. This is supported by local tradition, which identified Conachar Mór mac Aoidh, the progenitor of the clans Forbes, MacKay and Urquhart, as the owner of the castle in the late 12th century. This is likely to have been a fortification on the southern summit, the highest point of the site and the location of the earlier Pictish fort. Ancillary structures are likely to have been constructed where possible on the surrounding slopes. Such an arrangement would conform both to the format of motte-and-bailey castles being constructed at the time by the adherents of the Canmore kings and to the 'indigenous' traditions of fortification derived from forts and duns. Defences are likely to have been constructed from a combination of earth, timber and stone without mortar, but there is no direct evidence for occupation of the site in this period.

Phase 3 – The shell keep

The acquisition of Urquhart by Alan Durward in the late 1220s suddenly made it a possession of one of the most powerful men in the country, justiciar of Scotland, regent during the minority of Alexander III and owner of many other castles. The mortared walls around the southern summit (the area Simpson referred to as a motte) with their splayed base are clearly earlier than the walls that abut them. Parts of the walls have been rebuilt, in particular at the north end, which may have originally incorporated a small round tower. The structure thus created would appear to have provided a strong perimeter defence around the summit, within which timber and more lightly constructed buildings would be placed.

This development can be seen as a coming together of the shell keep (**8**) and the tradition of stone defences following the line of rock outcrops that

8 Ground plan of Urquhart showing suggested arrangement of Alan Durward's castle, mid-13th Century

was reaching its greatest strength on the western seaboard at castles like Dunstaffnage, Tioram and Mingary. Cruden dated this form of defensive structure to the first half of the 13th century, making an association with Alan Durward possible. The shell keep would have formed the core of a larger complex, with an outer defensive line provided by the cutting of the ditch to separate the castle area from the land to the west. A ditch of similar dimensions is also found at one of Durward's other castles, Coull on Deeside. Urquhart and Coull share similarities in their position – naturally protected on three sides, with a ditch cutting them off from gently rising ground – but neither ditch has been dated. The area thus defined by the ditch was presumably enclosed by a stout palisade.

Phase 4 – Curtain-walled castle

The next step in Urquhart's development seems to come before the end of the 13th century, probably when the castle was held by the powerful Comyn family. It seems to have been developed along similar lines to Kildrummy and Bothwell. Kildrummy and Bothwell (as originally planned) share an arrangement of a curtain wall, (**9**) a formidable gatehouse, a substantial great hall and a separate donjon tower positioned on the perimeter away from the most likely thrust of any attack. The gatehouse at Urquhart, a distinct block formed by two D-shaped halves flanking the central passage, seems to be a modest version of the more architecturally refined example at Kildrummy. The curtain wall on the landward side appears to be later than both the shell keep and the gatehouse, but the basement of the hall range overlooking the loch seems to be contemporary with its adjacent curtain walls. While the tower house has been subject to later changes, its lowest levels appear to be earlier than the curtain wall on the landward side but its precise order of building is unclear. The great hall was raised on a basement, to be level with the adjacent rock outcrop. A mass of masonry in the centre of this basement may represent a support for a central hearth or brazier in the hall above, which was otherwise floored in timber. The building on the northern tip of the site, which has been identified as a chapel, may date from this period also.

The arrangement at Urquhart of a new donjon tower, approached from a first floor entrance (the ditch in front of it is a product of the partial excavation of this area by the Ministry

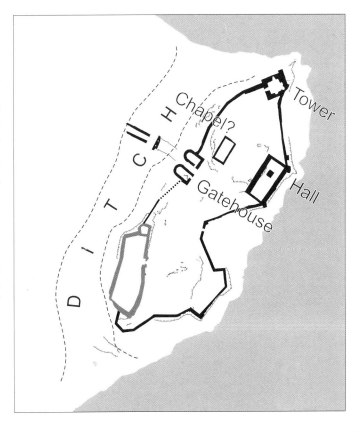

9 *Ground plan of Urquhart showing suggested alterations by the Comyns, late 13th Century*

of Works) and placed well back from the new double-drum gatehouse, echoes the grander structural arrangements at Kildrummy and Bothwell, which have been dated to the decades before the outbreak of war with England in the 1290s. While the visible structures at Urquhart contain very little dating evidence, there is nothing about their forms or details that would contradict a date in the late 13th century. The Comyn constructions of Lochindorb, Inverlochy and Balvenie show that this family was capable of sophisticated castle building and such a major investment in Urquhart, a new possession, would not be out of place at this time. Such an upgrading of Urquhart in the 1280s would go some way to explain why it was never taken by force. Its initial capture by the English in 1296 was presumably largely related to the nationwide Comyn capitulation, but it withstood a siege by Andrew de Moray in 1297, only fell to the English in 1303 once the starved garrison sallied forth in a fit of chivalry, and was one of only five castles in Scotland to withstand the invasion of Edward Balliol in 1333.

Phase 5 – Elaboration

The next phase of building at Urquhart appears to see a number of masonry buildings being added (**10**). These include the ranges either side of the hall and, possibly, the building thought to have housed a smithy to the south of the watergate. Simpson had assumed that the entirety of the crescent of buildings of which the hall formed the centre was, essentially, of a single date. However, the poor bonding against the hall block above the ground floor and the noticeably thinner construction of the east walls of the flanking structures, indicates that they are later. The return on the threshold of the doorway into what Simpson probably correctly identified as the kitchen would be consistent with a 14th-century date for this addition (**11**). Whether this aggrandizement should be attributed to the Randolphs in the first half of the century, the Crown in the 1340s and 1350s, the Earl of Sutherland before 1370 or the sons of Robert II in the last decades of the century it is difficult to be sure. However, these enlargements did not happen all at once, with further additions taking place at various times, including the construction of one of the most puzzling structures at Urquhart. Attached to the west end of the kitchen is a narrow extension with no openings that face the castle and with no evidence for flooring below

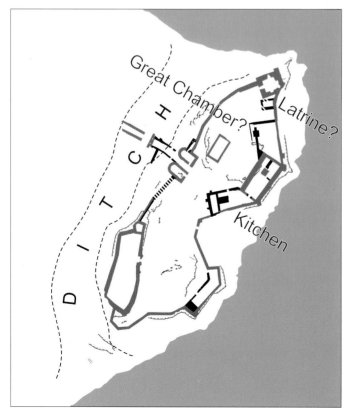

10 Ground plan of Urquhart showing additions probably made during the 14th Century

second floor level. Buttresses on its north and west walls give them the strength to stand without the bracing of a floor at first floor level. The only apparent opening from the space formed by these walls is into the area overlooking the bay, which is reached by the watergate. Clearly this building has a function related to the use of the loch but it is too high above the water to be a boathouse. It is possible that it could be a tall space for drying sails and nets, but without any similar structures elsewhere this remains merely speculation. Other additions suggested for this phase in the 14th century include the prison in the gatehouse, the thickening and heightening of the curtain wall between the gatehouse and the shell keep, the addition of screen walls between the gatehouse and the drawbridge, and the construction of a small tower adjacent to the keep, possibly to serve as a latrine tower.

Phase 6 – Repair following damage

The augmentation and additions of the 14th century seem to be followed by a period of quite drastic retrenchment, possibly following severe damage. The hall seems to have been reconstructed with slimmer walls than before and, possibly, a new spine wall running down its length. The block to its north, identified by Simpson as the 'Great Chamber', seems to have been abandoned, with a garderobe chute opening into what had been the basement. A similar arrangement of a garderobe chute disgorging a short distance above ground level within the walls of the castle is found on the motte, where new structures seem to have been constructed within the shell keep. This phase of reconstruction seems to have been instigated by considerable destruction and, with the reoccupation of the shell keep, to have been motivated by security concerns (**12**). It should be expected that the civil strife that surrounded the claims to the earldom of Ross took its toll on Urquhart, and it is tempting to see this phase of destruction and repair as dating to the very end of the 14th or the early 15th century. Indeed, the southern summit was the location of the many finds dating to

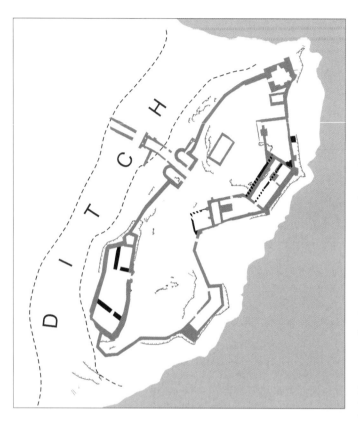

*12 Ground plan
of Urquhart showing
the alterations probably
made during the
15th Century*

the 15th century, including a fine bronze ewer, suggesting quite significant levels of occupation at this time. The discovery of so many finds suggests a rapid abandonment such as that caused by the sudden destruction of a building.

Phase 7 – The tower house

In 1509, the charter that awarded the barony of Urquhart to James Grant of Freuchie made it clear that building works at Urquhart were long overdue. Grant was required '*to repair or build at the Castle a tower, with an outwork or rampart of stone or lime, ... to construct within the Castle a hall, chamber and kitchen, with all other requisite offices, such as a pantry, bakehouse, brewhouse, barn, oxhouse, kiln, cot, dove-grove, and orchard.*' The extent of rebuilding required suggests that the castle was so much damaged as to be considered incapable of occupation let alone defence. However, Grant's needs and resources in the 16th century were very different from those of Durward or Thomas Randolph with their great baronial households 300 years before. It is therefore not surprising that Urquhart as rebuilt by the Grants was radically different. Adapting the 13th-century keep, Grant constructed a new tower house (**13**). Burying the lowest storey of this building, a small, level courtyard was formed using the remains of the earlier buildings to the south and a new building against the landward curtain. A dovecot was constructed towards the south end of the site and a wall seems to have been thrown across the site from the gatehouse across to the north side of the watergate. It was possibly as part of these works that the remaining walls of the other buildings within the circuit of the curtains were cast down into their own basements. Removing unwanted buildings from the north end of the site, the new, smaller core of the castle made good defensive sense, depriving would-be raiders from cover in the immediate vicinity of the new tower. It is possible also that the flattened buildings were intended to provide platforms for the defensive artillery, which was later stolen in the Great Raid of 1545. The tower house of the lairds of Freuchie was subject to later alterations but these did not change the overall planning or use of the site.

Summary

Such an interpretation of the remains at Urquhart is plagued with considerable uncertainty. It remains a theory and, by definition, is not proven; the evidence that supports it is corroboratory, not absolute. However, this narrative certainly fits better today's understanding of the development of castles in Scotland, and it accords better with what we know of the ebb and flow of power and peace in the Great Glen. It goes some way to explain some of the anomalies of the site: why a garderobe chute empties into the basement of what Simpson called the 'Great Chamber'; why the southern summit was so rich in 15th-century artefacts; and why 16th- and 17th-century artefacts seem to be restricted almost entirely to the tower house, its inner close and the gatehouse. It would also explain why, even in the earliest 18th-century views of the castle, so much of the medieval structure is missing.

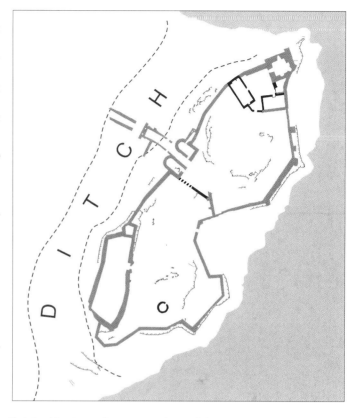

Scope

This book is not intended to be a detailed justification of a new reading of the development of Urquhart Castle. Nor is it intended to be a comprehensive history of the Great Glen; a single, slim volume could not do it justice. What this book does set out to do is tell the history of Urquhart Castle, placing it firmly in the context of its surroundings. In a history based on high politics, Urquhart will appear intermittently, as if blinking into existence when the gaze of the historian falls upon it. This book tries to give a history of Urquhart where the gaze remains on Urquhart and its place within the Great Glen. Over this long history the relationship between the castle and its immediate vicinity has constantly evolved. While Urquhart may not have been the hub of all the events in Glen Mór, standing watch on Strone Point it has been the Glen's most persistent witness.

13 *Ground plan of Urquhart showing the arrangements made by John Grant in the early 16th Century. The focus of the site is now restricted to the north end and many buildings were cleared*

[1] Simpson, W Douglas, *Urquhart Castle*, Transactions of the Gaelic Society of Inverness, 1930, p. 76.

2

The Great Glen before Urquhart

The Great Glen Fault

The Great Glen is not just a slice across Scotland; it is a slice straight through the Earth's crust reaching at least 40km (25 miles) down. What we now know as Scotland is made up of four slices of the Earth's surface that, over 400 million years ago, slowly slid their way past each other into something like their present positions. They are separated by three major fault lines, all of which run roughly south-west to north-east: the Southern Upland Fault, the Highland Boundary Fault and the Great Glen Fault. The Great Glen is the most dramatic of the three and is still the source of more earthquakes and tremors than anywhere else in Britain. The land to the north of the Great Glen is still slowly grinding its way westwards past the central Highlands. Estimates for how far a fault has moved are normally based on finding matching features on either side of the fault and measuring the displacement. However, the two sides of the Great Glen do not match in that way. While both sides are metamorphic rocks, they were formed far apart and have been brought together by movement along the Great Glen.

Currently it is thought that the fault has seen its sides move approximately 200km (124 miles) past each other. However, it is also worth bearing in mind that not all movement will have been in one direction. Most of the movement seems to have been *sinistral* (wherever you are standing, the land mass on the far side of the fault has been moving to the left). Some movements may have gone in the other direction and there is also evidence that the south side of the fault, particularly around the Moray Firth, has dropped in height. This area is also the recipient of later sedimentary rock known as 'old red sandstone'. This is softer than the metamorphic rocks along the rest of the Glen, resulting in a smoother, lower lying topography towards the Moray Firth.

Glaciation

As the rocks either side of the fault have been grinding past each other they have created a band of crushed rock along the fracture, which has been exploited by rivers as they make their way to the sea. At the height of the last Ice Age, between 22,000 and 18,000 years ago, the ice sheets covered the whole of Scotland, probably leaving the summits of only a few mountains such as the Cuillins on Skye to stand proud of the ice. The land beneath the sheet though was not amorphous; its glens directed the flow of ice and were enlarged by these glaciers. The ice cap was at its thickest over Rannoch Moor, from which ice seems to have flowed over into the Great Glen and north-east to the Moray Firth. The geological fault provided a line of weakness that

was exploited by the steady scouring of the glaciers. It was glaciation that smoothed the sides of the Great Glen; it was glaciation that deposited the gravels on which Fort Augustus and Inverness were built; and it was glaciation that grated away the softer rock to expose Strone Point, a small knoll that juts into Loch Ness on which would be built Urquhart Castle.

The first steps in the Great Glen

About 10,000 years ago the first people saw the Great Glen. As they travelled up the coasts of Britain in small hide-covered boats or log-canoes, either mouth of the Glen would have represented an easy route into the interior of the country. The evidence we have for these hunter-gatherer communities is slight. Their camps are unlikely to have seen permanent occupation as they followed patterns of movement and activity that were influenced by the seasons and the availability of food and other resources. The evidence we have for these peoples is largely confined to the coastal areas. There are two reasons for this: the shoreline, whose resources of fish and shellfish fluctuated little with the seasons, provided a useful buffer against the wide varieties of plenty and dearth further inland, and the enormous piles of shell that are associated with these maritime camps provided a micro-environment which has helped the preservation of other material, such as bone, which would have decayed in the acid soils further inland.

Mesolithic sites have been found at either end of the Great Glen, both in the Inverness area and widely scattered across the western seaboard. Excavations beneath

15 Carved stone ball found near Loch Lochy, now in the National Museum of Scotland. It is thought to date to between 3200 and 2500 BC

13–24 Castle Street, Inverness revealed a large amount of worked flint, a little shell, some red deer bone and a hearth that was dated to about 5000 BC (**14**). It is possible that the site had seen more than one phase of occupation, which would be consistent with the regular movement of people, exploiting different resources at different times of year. The large amount of worked flint (over 4,500 pieces) is a reminder that these camps are not all identical, with certain activities taking place in particular places at discrete times of the year.

On the other side of the River Ness, at Muirtown, another excavated site contained no worked stone but did reveal a series of shell deposits (predominantly oyster but also mussel and cockle) left by people collecting shellfish along the coast but, apparently, not fishing. The site is thought to date to the middle of the 4th millennium BC, significantly later than the Castle Street site, but like the earlier site, Muirtown contained red deer remains, in this case antler. It would appear that for the hunter-gatherers of the Mesolithic period the Great Glen may have offered easy access to those resources, such as deer bone, antler and hides, which supplemented what was available to them nearer the coasts. Without any finds from the Great Glen itself it is unclear how far these people may have ventured from the coasts but, given that they seem to have moved around the western seaboard by boat, it is likely that some of them, at least, will have crossed the country by the lochs and rivers of Glen Mór.

First farming and settlement

If evidence for Mesolithic activity in the Great Glen is sparse, the situation improves a little for the farmers who succeeded them. The landscape that had supported the hunter-gatherers was heavily wooded, with a mixture of birch, oak and hazel towards either end of the Glen but with an increasing proportion of pine at the expense of oak and hazel further inland. The woodland cover was not absolute and open spaces would have been created by rivers, bogs, rock outcrops and hilltops. While there is some evidence that hunter-gatherers in Scotland managed some woodland as a natural resource, for example to encourage hazel growth, it was farming that provided the impetus for the clearance of the woodland.

In the Great Glen, the homes of these first farmers have not been located, nor have any of the ritual structures associated with them. However, a number of cup-marked rocks across the well-drained, south-facing slopes of Glenurquhart indicate their presence (**15**). Two stone axes have also been found near Garbeg, as well as a very fine polished axe at Borlum (**16**). This sort of axe would appear to be associated with status rather than being a functional tool. The stone for such axes often came from as far afield as mainland Europe. Such long distance contacts are surprisingly common at this time and so it is not particularly remarkable to find a carved stone ball at Loch Lochy – a ritual (or ornamental) object, usually associated with north-east Scotland.

16 Polished stone axe found on Borlum Farm in 1892 now in Inverness Museum and Art Gallery

Elaborate burial

Hunter-gatherer communities have often been characterized by a lack of hierarchy and the earliest farmers appear to have had similar communal attitudes, with the first tombs being used communally for shared ancestors. However with time, hierarchies seem to have developed, with tombs being focused on key individuals.

The cairn at Corrimony (**17**) was apparently constructed to take a single crouched burial. When excavated in 1952, while the body had dissolved completely, the stain left by its decomposition could still be seen (**18**). The cairn at Corrimony is one of a group of similar cairns known as 'clava cairns' after the site to the east of Inverness where they were first described. Another example, in a poorer state of preservation, survives at Carn Daley, near Balnagrantach. The clava cairns are characterized by a passageway entering the cairn from the south-west, possibly linked to the movement of the moon, and a circle of stones around the cairn. The clava cairns form a fairly tight group around the Moray Firth and, while the worship connected with heavenly

18 The pattern of staining of found on the floor of Corrimony Chambered Cairn when it was excavated in 1952. Although the body had decayed completely, its crouched position could still be seen in the stains left by decomposition

22

elements was widespread, the Bronze Age is characterized by an increasing regional variation of monuments. For the first time it is possible to detect cultural differences between the people living around the Great Glen: those at the north-east end of the Glen have closer cultural links with their neighbours around the Moray Firth than with those people living at the south-west end of Glen Mór.

It is perhaps a mark of the success of the farming community in Glenurquhart that, in addition to the stone axes, other high-status goods have been found in the glen. Some of them, such as bronze axes, have been stray finds while the excavation of the burial cairn at Balnalick revealed a pot, some fragments of human bone and a very elegant bronze razor (**19**).

Settlement and defence

The transition from the Neolithic period of the first farmers to the Bronze Age was a gradual one, where the use of bronze was simply one element of the changes. Similarly, the end of the Bronze Age after c.700 BC is marked by more than just the introduction of iron but there are also strong elements of continuity. The sharpest change seems to come in the sphere of religious belief, with a shift away from worship of a heavenly divinity towards more terrestrial concerns, water in particular, and a similar abandonment of the great ritual monuments. However, from this period we have a wealth of evidence of settlement. The roundhouses that are found in abundance across the Highlands seem to have originated in the late Bronze Age and represent an important element of continuity. A large number of these houses are to be found above Glenurquhart, north of Garbeg and Culnakirk. Known today as hut circles, these round circular houses were impressive buildings, sometimes of two storeys and often larger than many modern houses. The sites also contain numerous

19 Pot and razor found in a cist in a cairn at Balnalick in Glenurquhart in the 1880s. The pot held fragments of human bone and the razor but crumbled during excavation. The razor is now in Inverness Museum and Art Gallery

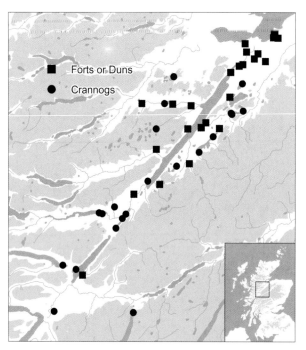

burnt mounds along the side of the Culnakirk Burn. These mounds are piles of heat-affected rock that seem to have been used to heat water for cooking or possibly bathing.

However, the array of hut circles strewn across the hills above Glenurquhart does not represent the totality of Iron-Age settlement in the Great Glen. The Iron Age has been differentiated from earlier prehistory by an increase in warfare, and it is true that this period does see a proliferation of defensive structures (**20**). Those at the north-east end of the Great Glen, such as Craig Phadrig near Inverness, Craig Mony in Glenurquhart, Dun Dearduil and Castle Kitchie above the River Farigaig on the south side of Loch Ness, all seem to relate to a pattern of hilltop fort building that is found across southern and eastern Scotland. Torr Dhuinn, above Fort Augustus, seems to be more closely related to the tradition

20 Fort, duns and crannogs in the Great Glen. These sites were constructed over many centuries and were not all occupied at the same time

of duns found on the western seaboard. Both the forts and the duns seem to have shared techniques of construction, such as timber-laced stone walling, but while the forts seem to have enclosed groups of buildings, duns appear to be more concentrated fortifications; strongly built sub-circular buildings, often with additional structures attached to them.

Hilltops were clearly chosen for their defensive qualities and their visibility as signifiers of dominion over an area. Craig Mony, commanding the confluence of the Enrick and the Coiltie rivers in Glenurquhart is a good example of this. However, the qualities of defence and visibility were also shared by crannogs. These artificial islands are found through the north and west of Scotland. With a form clearly related to roundhouses, crannogs were constructed on massive timber piles driven into the loch-bed, often supplemented by large amounts of dumped rock. The depth of Loch Ness means that only one crannog, Cherry Island or Eilean Muireach, seems to have been built on it. However, the shallower waters of Loch Oich contain several crannogs, as do many other subsidiary lochs that feed into Glen Mór.

By the start of the 1st millennium AD, the Great Glen can be seen as having a structure of settlement that would be familiar to later generations – farms situated on the better agricultural land, strongholds positioned at prominent locations, and a graduated distinction discernible between one end of Glen Mór and the other.

3

The fort – the 1st millennium AD

The emergence of the Great Glen into recorded history took place slowly. The people of Glen Mór in the 1st millennium AD left no written accounts so our earliest information comes in the form of scraps from other sources. These sources themselves are varied and are not always reliable; it is probably fair to say that every source for the history of this period is, to some extent, partial, partisan and contradicted somewhere else. They do not provide us with a coherent history of the Great Glen but rather a series of fragments, between which there are many gaps that need to be filled by informed deduction and a little supposition.

Over the course of the 1st millennium much changed. Most perceptions of northern Scotland at this time are dominated by thoughts of the Picts, but this thousand years in the Great Glen neither begins nor ends with them; their ancestors, the Caledones, confronted the Romans, and the Scots of Dál Riata challenged the Picts for control of the mainland. The Norse attacks from the late 8th century changed the political map of what would become Scotland and produced a new great power in the north, the Mormaers of Moray.

The written sources for this period include the geographical work of Ptolemy of Alexandria in the 2nd century AD, a wide range of monastic documents from Britain and Ireland, the Pictish king lists, British and Irish poems, Norse sagas and the writings of scholars such as the Venerable Bede and St Adomnán, the biographer of St Columba. None of these documents sought to describe places or events in the Great Glen in particular although the activities of St Columba mean that the Great Glen is mentioned several times by Adomnán. It is only by testing these sources against each other and against evidence from archaeology and place names that we can grope towards an understanding of the Great Glen's long dawn of history.

Who were the Caledones?

The Caledones are the first people with a name that we can associate with the Great Glen. In the middle of the 2nd century AD Ptolemy of Alexandria sought to present the compiled knowledge of the Roman Empire in an Atlas of the World. While the shape of Ptolemy's map of Scotland was distorted, it is still possible to identify many of the rivers, headlands and other places (**21**). North of the Forth-Clyde line Ptolemy distributed the names of twelve tribes around the various parts of his map of Scotland.

While it is worth remembering that a map of Scotland prepared in Egypt from Roman sources will be full of inaccuracies, it would appear that at this time the Great Glen was within the territory of the Caledones. This tribe is thought to have given

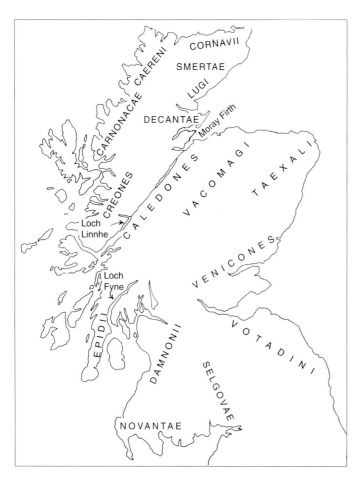

21 The distribution of late iron-age tribes in Scotland according to Ptolemy of Alexandria

its name to Dunkeld, 'Fortress of the Caledonians', which suggests that their territory dominated the central Highlands. However, the territories and boundaries are vague and the south-west end of the Glen could have fallen into the territory of the Creones or the Epidii, with the north-east end abutting the lands of the Decantæ. Given the differences between the two ends of the Great Glen, which are evident in the construction of burial cairns and forts, it is perhaps unlikely that the Caledones had homogenous dominion over the entire length of the Glen. We have little other information about these Highland tribes, although the fact that, according to Tacitus, they could present a united army of 30,000 men at their defeat by the Romans at Mons Graupius in AD 83 suggests that they were not so disparate as to fail to unite in the face of a common enemy.

By the end of the 2nd century this coalition, which may have been novel in AD 83, appears to have become established. Dio Cassius, in his *History of Rome*, gives an account of the campaigns of Emperor Septimius Severus in Britain in which he tells us that in AD 197 the Caledones had breached a treaty with Rome by helping in the defence of their southern neighbours, the Maeatae. The term 'Caledones' now appears to refer to the unified Highland tribes, with the Maeatae occupying Angus and Fife. The assumption has been that this rapid unification of tribes came about as a result of the threat posed by Rome, since there is nothing to imply that a war of conquest was fought between the various tribes during the 2nd century.

The Caledones in the Great Glen

The Caledones of the end of the 3rd century AD were essentially still an Iron Age people; they grew out of the tribes of the first millennium BC rather than ousting them and therefore are likely to have had similar social structures and belief systems to the numerous tribes that the Romans first encountered. This evolution makes it difficult to make firm distinctions between sites of this period and earlier Iron Age sites without excavation. In other parts of Scotland, the late Iron Age has been seen as a time of agricultural expansion, with the great forts losing their importance and individual farmsteads becoming more elaborate. Clearly, agricultural expansion in the Great Glen is likely to have been more limited than in areas such as Lothian or Angus, but with sites such as Craig Phadrig apparently abandoned at this time, this general trend may well have been repeated in the Highlands.

The Great Glen does not appear to have been touched directly by the Roman occupation of Britain. While Roman artefacts have been found in the Great Glen (the occasional coin around Inverness, a 1st-century hinged brooch from near Dores) these are part of the normal circulation of valuable, portable goods beyond the limits of the Empire through trade, gifts and raiding. Of more interest is the find, in 1767, on the site of the defences of Fort Augustus of *'an earthen urn, of a blue colour, with about 300 pieces of coin, of mixed metal, some a little larger than our halfpence, and the others the size of farthings'*. The army officer who described the find thought that all the coins were from the reign of Diocletian (AD 284–305). Sadly the hoard is no longer traceable and we have no idea of what context it was in. However, two comparable hoards at Birnie, south of Elgin, have been found within a prosperous Iron-Age settlement and have been interpreted as Roman bribes, buried either for security or for ritual purposes, as offerings or talismans.

Ritual deposits, especially involving water, were commonly practised by Iron-Age peoples, among whom the Caledones must be counted. Their belief systems appear to have imbued water with divine significance and these beliefs survived until the arrival of Christianity and even for some time beyond this. Adomnán, in describing Columba's missionary work, refers to the beliefs of some of those in the Great Glen whom the saint met, and they often involve water: the River Lochy was referred to as the Black Goddess; a spring was worshipped by the Picts because of its powers to cripple, blind

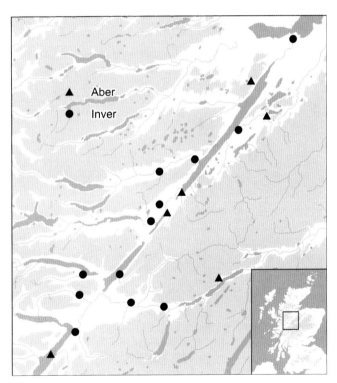

22 Place names in the Great Glen which incorporate 'aber' or 'inver' elements

and cause leprosy. It is therefore not entirely surprising to find that places with the Pictish term 'aber-', a confluence or river mouth, may have had pagan, spiritual significance. The Great Glen has at least three aber- place names, Abriachan on Loch Ness, Aberchalder at the north end of Loch Oich and Lochaber (the loch of the river mouths), which originally referred to Loch Linnhe between Inverlochy and Corran. However, aber- is a Pictish name form and it is quite possible that many more of these aber- place names have been replaced by the Gaelic equivalent, 'inver-' (**22**).

Chroniclers of Iron-Age Europe record how the Celtic peoples of Gaul worshipped in sanctuaries focused on natural features such as springs, lakes or groves. There is no reason to suppose that the Caledones were so very different. One of these sanctuaries is still identifiable in the Great Glen, at Temple in Glenurquhart. The modern name of the site is an anglicization of the Gaelic *An Teampull* (chapel) but the name of the hill above it tells an older story. Creag Nay or Neimhidh, the rock of the Nemed (noble sanctuary) takes its name from the pre-Christian sanctuary at its foot, later taken over for the first Christian foundation in Glenurquhart. As a remarkable example of the longevity of unwritten local religious practice, a clootie or rag well (**25**) and two elderly ash trees (**23**) on the site were still venerated by local people seeking cures for ailments as late as 1885, a possible echo of the site's pre-Christian worship.

During the 4th century, as the power of Rome in Britain weakened, these unified tribes did not fracture as the threat from their common enemy receded, but rather continued to consolidate, at first forming two groups north of the Forth–Clyde line, probably divided by the hills of the Mounth. By the second half of the 4th century, the Romans often refer to a single people living beyond the Empire's northern border, the Picts, who were a union of the former tribes.

23 The two ash trees at Temple stood next to the holy well which was destroyed when the road was widened in the late 19th Century.

Pictish Airchartdan

The first written record of most sites is normally fairly mundane – a mention in a charter or a passing reference in a list of other places. The first appearance for Urquhart is, by way of contrast, heralded by angels. St Columba, the man who is credited with bringing Christianity to the Northern Picts, travelled through the Great Glen on his missionary journeys in the AD 570s. On one occasion he was inspired by the Holy Ghost to make a detour to Airchartdan where a man '*who hath preserved his natural goodness through all his life, even to extreme old age*' was on the point of death. The angels were ready to take the old man's soul up to Heaven but were waiting for Columba to baptize him. St Adomnán, writing at the end of the 7th century, tells us that Emchath, the old man on his deathbed, was baptized by Columba, as was his son, Virolec, and their entire household (**26**). The name 'Urquhart' or 'Urchardainn', or 'Airchartdan' in Adomnán's *Life of St Columba*, was established by the middle of the 6th century and can be translated as meaning 'by the wood or thicket', features that to the Picts are likely to have been the distinguishing characteristics of the area.

The first hint that the site of Urquhart Castle was occupied well before the foundation of the later medieval castle came at the turn of the 20th century, when Lt. Col. A B M'Hardy identified vitrified material among the beach shingle at the castle. This melted stone came from the destruction of timber-laced ramparts, which were a feature of defended sites in both the Iron Age and the Pictish period. However, it was not until the early 1980s that archaeological excavation confirmed that Urquhart had been occupied possibly as early as the 5th century AD. Four trenches were laid out focusing on the highest part of the castle site, the southern summit, where the staff of the Ministry of Works had reported vitrified material in the 1920s. Sealed beneath large quantities of later medieval material were found the remains of occupation that had come to a sudden end by fire in the late 11th or early 12th century. The construction of the later medieval walls on the summit had disturbed the earlier remains, but, even though only a small proportion of the summit was exposed, it was possible to identify at least two timber buildings with cobbled floors and central hearths built against the inner face of a stone rampart that followed the lines of the later wall around the summit. Interestingly, other than a broken quern used in the cobbling, no artefacts were found that were attributable to the period of this Pictish fort, making it impossible to say very much about the activities on the site.

High status sites occupied over this period, such as Dunadd in Argyll (**24**)

24 *Reconstruction view of Dunadd showing the nucleated fort with a series of terraced subdivisions below the core of the fort on the summit*

26 *Columba baptising Emchath on his deathbed*

and Dundurn in Perthshire, are characterized by a defended summit around which developed a larger complex arranged on terraces spreading down the slopes. With no artefacts from Urquhart at this period to confirm its status, it is unwise to draw too strong a parallel with these other sites, but the topography of Urquhart would lend itself to this treatment. When trying to imagine Pictish Urquhart we must also remember that the ditch had not yet been sliced across the headland and that the defensive qualities of the north end of the site, therefore, would have been less pronounced. Clearly, if Urquhart remained in occupation for another four centuries after Emchath, then there was plenty of opportunity for the expansion of activity on the site, but in the absence of further excavation this remains unclear.

Who was Emchath?

Adomnán tells us very little about Emchath. It has always been assumed that the reference to the estate of Airchartdan and Emchath's household would imply that he was the leading figure of the estate, such as its owner or keeper.

Pictland was divided into provinces, each ruled by a *regulus* or sub-king. Such a system of delegation was a necessity to provide any level of control over an area that, at times, seems to have covered much of modern Scotland. These provinces, in their turn, seem to have been divided into estates, each in the control of a local potentate such as Emchath. On the basis of later evidence in the south of Pictland, these estates seem to have followed a fairly typical pattern. An estate would have covered a large variety of land, extending from good agricultural land up to high pastures in the hills. The essential components of an estate were a principal residence, a meeting place for administration and justice, a ritual (later an ecclesiastical) centre and a number of agricultural subdivisions or portions of the estate. Such a model of estate management would fit what we know of Glenurquhart in this period, with the fort at Urquhart Castle as the principal residence. Of the agricultural subdivisions, the only one that is still identifiable is Pitkerrald ('Cyril's portion'). This place name may be a relic of one of several such farms, consisting of the main farm settlement and possibly outlying houses occupied by tied tenants.

Arguments have been made that the post of thane (an individual appointed to manage an estate, often for a fixed period), which first appears in the 12th century, was an evolution of the post of *toísech*, an older Pictish rank. If this is the case, then it would imply that there are likely to have been similarities in the status and purpose of the position (**27**). On this basis it is possible that Emchath,

27 Pictish silver chain found in 1809 during the construction of the Caledonian Canal at Torvean, near Inverness. The function of such an expensive and conspicuous object is not known. The chain is now in the National Museum of Scotland

as a local leader, held his position as a royal appointment rather than as of right. While Emchath's son Virolec may well have become the next *toísech*, this quite possibly would have been on the basis of an official appointment rather than inheritance.

The Great Glen in Emchath's day

28 The territories of the Picts, the Scots of Dál Riata and other groups in the mid 6th Century AD

Tradition has it that at the start of the 6th century Fergus Mór mac Eirc, a Scot from Ireland, founded the territory of Dál Riata, covering an area roughly equivalent to modern Argyll. The Dalriadan territories appear to have been bounded to the east by the Druim Alban (the ridge of mountains that stretch from Loch Lomond north up to Sutherland), and to have stretched from the Firth of Clyde to the River Shiel (**28**). The Druim Alban is pierced by many valleys but the Great Glen, navigable for almost its entire length by small boats, such as hide-bound *currachs*, was the most direct crossing through the Druim Alban between Dál Riata and Pictland. Glen Mór was both an easy route between the two kingdoms and a gaping gateway in their respective boundaries.

St Columba's mission to the Northern Picts was focused in particular on one individual: Bridei son of Mailcon, the king of the Picts from AD c.550–c.583. Bridei (or Brude) is the first Pictish king about whom we have more information than just a name in one of the Pictish king lists. Until recently it had been thought that Bridei had his principal fortress at Inverness, making him unique among the 'historic' Pictish kings in that he ruled Pictland from north of the Mounth. Recent research suggests that, in fact, Bridei may have had his prime residence near the Tay. However, Bridei's territory was extensive; it seems to have included the Pictish heartland in the east, as far south as the Tay, north to Orkney and possibly west as far as Skye. After his defeat of the Dalriadan Scots in AD 558/9, it is possible that he also considered Dál Riata to be a vassal state.

A realm of this extent would be well served by a base at Inverness, even if it was not the royal seat. Inverness was supplied with good agricultural land, open sea routes to the east and north and direct access through the Great Glen to the western seaboard beyond the Druim Alban. The precise location of Bridei's fort above the River Ness has been a matter of speculation, with both Craig Phadrig and the site of Inverness Castle being suggested. However, excavations by the Inverness Local History Forum in 2004 have helped identify another strong candidate at Auldcastle, on the hill called the Crown in Inverness. (This is also thought to have been the site of MacBeth's castle in the 11th century) (**29**). The fact that Columba met Bridei at Inverness rather than further south may stem from Columba's focus on Northern Pictland, the ease of travel across Scotland through the Great Glen or simply a matter of the most convenient place to meet as Bridei moved around his realm.

The territory of the Scots at the south-west end of the Great Glen was controlled by the Cenél Loairn, one of three major related kinship groupings among the Scots of Dál Riata. The Cenél nGabráin, who provided most of the kings of Dál Riata, held the southern half of Argyll, the Cenél n-Oengusa held Islay and the Cenél Loairn held Lorn, Lochaber, Mull, Morvern, Coll and Tiree, with their main fortress probably at Dunollie, near Oban. The territories of Knapdale and mid-Argyll seem to have fluctuated between the Cenél Loairn and the Cenél nGabráin in their rivalry for the kingship, a position that was only successfully held by the Cenél Loairn for a few decades at the start of the 8th century.

The evidence for the Cenél Loairn occupation in the south-west end of the Glen is difficult to identify. Dalriadan place names are largely indistinguishable from later Gaelic place names because they derive from the same root. However, the western seaboard historically has been dominated by consideration of its seaways. In such a context we should probably expect that the south-west end of the Great Glen, with comparatively little good farmland, would not have been strongly incorporated into the territories of the Cenél Loairn.

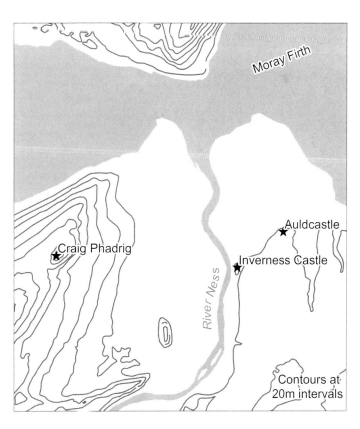

29 The area around the mouth of the River Ness showing three sites which have been suggested as being the fort of Bridei, son of Mailcon.

The picture that emerges of the Great Glen in this period is of a major centre of authority at Inverness, with Pictish estates extending down Loch Ness. The rural Highlands have always been heavily reliant on livestock and cattle would have been not just the foundation of the economy but also significant symbols of wealth and status. The other resource that the Great Glen possessed was timber. Emchath's estate and other locations in the Glen had good natural resources of timber. These forests were made easier to exploit by the ease of transport provided by the long lochs of the Glen. Inevitably, with timber as a key resource for the area, a certain level of woodland management should be expected. Research in association with the excavation of Buiston crannog in Ayrshire (dating from the 6th to 7th centuries AD) suggested that the exploitation of the woodland was carried out in a manner that avoided the overexploitation of any one area or resource. Clearly Ayrshire is a long way from the Great Glen, but we know from Adomnán that timber for Iona was sourced on the mainland with large timbers taken down lochs, waterways and even across stretches of sea towed behind boats as small as the humble *currachs*. This level of effort that went into sourcing timber reflects its importance, and the care shown in woodland management in contemporary Ayrshire would be entirely consistent with the value timber supplies had in the Highlands at this time.

Beyond the south end of Loch Ness, the lesser availability of good agricultural land, combined with the uncertainties of living near a poorly defined border, resulted in a transitional zone with few obvious and immovable signs of status. Such border zones are often subject to unrest and, while the major clashes between the Dalriadan Scots and the Picts may have taken place further south, much of the Great Glen is likely to have been subject to minor raiding and a degree of lawlessness. Columba was followed in this area by 'hostile pursuers', who burnt down a village on the shore of Loch Lochy where they believed the saint and his companions were sleeping. The presence at Bridei's court of both hostages and Irish slaves indicates the martial ruthlessness of 6th-century society and constant skirmishing is likely to have been part of normal life in Glen Mór.

However, what distinguished the Great Glen was not that it contained a boundary but that it formed a route across the boundary. This made the Glen a principal artery not just for trading cargoes, which could be carried on the extensive stretches of water of the Great Glen, but also of ideas, fashions and philosophies. The movement of people and commodities along the Glen would have been a common occurrence in the 6th century. There would have been an awareness that Glen Mór linked two separate realms, that to go from one end of the Great Glen to the other was to go to a foreign land, with a different language, different beliefs and different rulers.

The mission of St Columba

Over the course of the 6th and 7th centuries the greatest changes in the Great Glen were not social or political but religious. The appearance, probably some time in the AD 570s, of St Columba and his companions making their way to Inverness was not remarkable in itself, but the changes that stemmed from this mission were both major and permanent.

Bede states that Columba's aim was to convert the Northern Picts, although Adomnán's account is surprisingly short on evangelism. Bridei son of Mailcon was presumably already acquainted with Christianity, given that it was already firmly, if not exclusively, established in the southern half of Pictland. Columba's mission seems to be less concerned with conversion than with diplomacy. He was a member of the Irish aristocracy, a figure of sufficient influence that he could direct the course of succession to the Dalriadan kingship. The arrival of such a figure at the Pictish court clearly had a diplomatic importance greater than that of a mere wandering cleric.

Bridei himself appears only rarely in Adomnán's account of Columba's activities at the Pictish court. The saint's great adversary was not the king, who from Columba's first arrival '*greatly honoured the holy and venerable man, as was fitting, with high esteem*', but rather Broichan, the foster-father of the king and the Picts' most influential 'magician'. Broichan seems to embody the resistance of North Pictish beliefs to the arrival of Christianity, raising a storm on Loch Ness against Columba and presenting constant hostility to the missionaries.

Broichan's status as foster-father of the king marks the political importance of the Pictish priesthood, and he played a role of adviser and legitimator for the Pictish throne very similar to that of Columba for the Dalriadan throne. Columba's mission to Bridei was less one of religious conversion and more one of seeking Bridei's permission for the Christian church to function in North Pictland. Indeed, Adomnán only records one direct discussion between Bridei and Columba and this is, essentially, a secular matter, concerning Columba's request that Bridei order the *regulus* of Orkney to permit the safe passage of one Cormac, described as a soldier of Christ.

Holy water

The acceptance of Christianity as an alternative to the pre-existing beliefs of the Northern Picts was greatly helped by a shared set of cultural references. While Columba defeated Broichan's magic with stronger Christian magic as he sailed down Loch Ness, against the storm raised by the Pictish magician, this was not simply a case of Columba beating Broichan at his own game. In one story, Columba went to the River Ness from which he took a white stone that could float in water and cure any ailment, but which would vanish when sought to cure someone whose time had come to die. In that the story concerns Columba controlling magical powers that are associated with a river, it would happily sit in an account of the work of a pagan wizard. While the creeds of the Christians and the Picts differed greatly, they both associated divinity with water and springs.

Adomnán recounted two particular stories that illustrate well the defeat of the Pictish magicians and their gods. When Columba encountered the malignant well worshipped by the Picts, he blessed it, washed in it and drank from it. From that time on, the well, said to be Fuaran Cholumchille at Invermoriston, was said to have curative powers and was venerated as such.

The second story clearly belongs to the realm of myth and its value to Adomnán must have lain in its symbolic value. Columba and his companions came across the funeral of a man who was killed by a water beast while swimming in the River Ness. Columba ordered one of his number, Lugne mocu Min, to swim across the river to fetch a boat. This disturbance in the water roused the beast, which appeared '*with gaping mouth and great roaring*' and was within '*the length of one short pole*' from the monk when Columba, making the sign of the Cross in the air, ordered the beast back and it fled '*as if pulled back with ropes*'. These two stories seem to show Christianity's defeat of Pictish water gods, a point that, Adomnán recounts, was not lost on the pagan onlookers, who promptly '*magnified the God of the Christians*'.

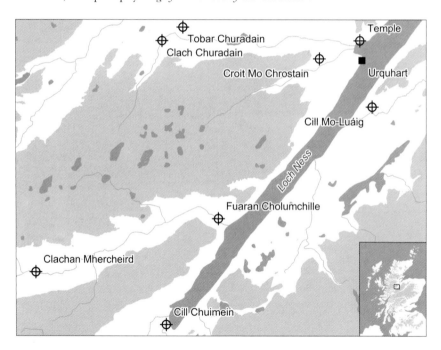

30 *Places in the Great Glen associated with early missionary saints*

Conversion of the masses

Once Columba had created a safe context in which it was possible for proselytizing to take place, it appears to have been others who converted the inhabitants of the Great Glen to Christianity. Mo-Luác, a contemporary of Columba, is of particular interest here as the founder of a monastery on Lismore at the mouth of Loch Linnhe and, according to legend, at both Mortlach in Aberdeenshire and at Rosemarkie on the Black Isle. The establishment of monasteries in the heart of Northern Pictland would have been impossible without Columba's diplomatic work and provided the basis for missions of conversion.

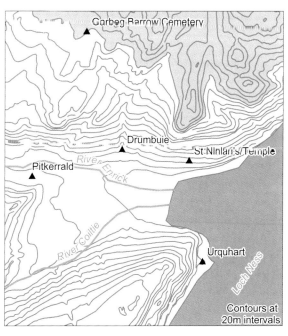

Excavations by the University of York at Tarbat in Easter Ross are giving us a clearer picture of the character of these new establishments. Tarbat (or Portmahomack) is the site of a substantial settlement based on a monastery, which, judging by the date of the earliest graves, seems to have been founded in the later 6th century. This date has led to the suggestion that Tarbat may have been founded by Columba himself. It was certainly founded about the time of Columba's journey to Inverness and it may have been that the foundation of such monasteries was the aim of the saint's discussions with king Bridei. The monumental sculpture from Tarbat displays clear links with contemporary work on Iona, and the evidence for the production of vellum, fine parchment, suggests that, like its mother-house, Tarbat was a centre of scholarship and had a scriptorium.

31 Places in Glenurquhart with Pictish remains or placenames

The line of communication between Iona and Tarbat runs straight down the Great Glen. It was the obvious route for Columba and his contemporaries to use. Given Mo-Luác's activities on both sides of the country it is not surprising to find references to him in the place names of the Glen. Near Ballaggan, north-west of Inverfarigaig stood the church of *Cill Mo-Luáig* and the adjacent land of *Croit Mo-Luáig* (**30**).

Other parts of the Great Glen regard other, less well-known figures as the first to bring the gospel to their area. Glenmoriston, in addition to the well and burial ground dedicated to Columba at Invermoriston, has, 15km (9 miles) further up the glen near Balintombuie, *Suidh Mhercheird* (Erchard's seat), *Fuaran Mhercheird* (Erchard's well) and *Clachan Mhercheird*, where this obscure figure is said to have built his church. Glenmoriston was not alone in staking a proprietorial claim to a missionary monk. Urquhart was distinguished from other places of the same name as *Urchudainn Mo Chrostain* (St Drostan's Urquhart). It is not clear whether Drostan, who may have founded religious houses at Aberdour and Deer, preached in Glenurquhart but his relics (possibly a cross) were held by a *deoir* or custodian at the chapel at St Ninians or Temple and his name appeared at *Croit Mo Chrostain* (St Drostan's Croft), a plot of land to the west of the site of Balmacaan House (**31**).

The impact of these gradual waves of missionary conversion was to change the Great Glen profoundly. The previous form of worship was essentially bound to natural features, with religious observance entwined with everyday life and with the

32 Whitebridge square barrow cemetery

entire landscape imbued with sanctity, although with particular locations being the focus of veneration. The Columban Church, with Christianity's emphasis on formal worship, adopted many of the sanctuaries and springs that had been special places of pagan belief as the sites of the new churches and chapels. This adoption may stem simply from both faiths sharing a reverence for springs and similar features, but it would also be expedient to build the new church at the established focal point for the spiritual life of the surrounding inhabitants. The construction of the appropriated site at Temple is a notable example of this, but the adoption of Christian attributions for springs such as Fuaran Cholumchille at Invermoriston and Tobar Churadain at Buntait in Glenurquhart are an integral part of this wider overlaying of pagan sites with Christian dedications.

33 Reconstruction of a burial at Garbeg

However, the picture of a succession of missionary saints swiftly translating pagan worship into Christian observance does not allow for the potential complexity of people's beliefs. The square barrow cemetery at Garbeg sits in the hills about 2km (1¼

miles) north of Drumnadrochit. It is one of two such cemeteries identified in the Great Glen, the other being near Whitebridge (**32**). Several others have been found further east but nowhere outside the Great Glen do these cemeteries survive as visible features in the landscape. In 1974 the owner of Garbeg Farm unearthed fragments of a symbol stone from the centre of what proved to be a round barrow (**33**). These most quintessentially Pictish monuments are rough-hewn stones

34 The Knocknagael Boar Stone, now in the offices of Highland Council in Inverness

decorated with a selection of symbols, which seem to be drawn from an accepted canon (**34**). Further examination of the surrounding ground showed that this barrow was part of a cemetery covering roughly 5,000m² (54,000ft²) with over twenty barrows still upstanding. The fragment, bearing the common Pictish symbol of a crescent and V-rod, is, by analogy with a similar grave at Dairy Park, Dunrobin, thought to date to the second half of the 7th century (**35**). Two other stones had been found near Drumbuie in 1864, between Drumnadrochit and Temple Pier, and were said to have come from a '*cist like structure*' (**36**). One of these stones is marked with a

35 Fragments of symbol stone found at Garbeg now in the Inverness Museum and Art Gallery

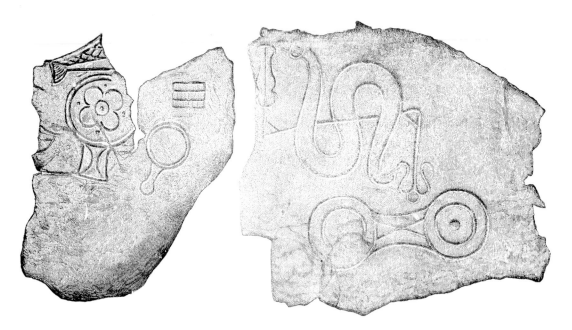

*36 Fragments
of symbol stones
found at Drumbuie*

serpent with a z-rod and a double disc, while the other has a mirror and comb, a circular disc with a rectangle and part of a salmon.

These symbol-bearing slabs have no Christian symbolism on them, which suggests either that the spread of the new faith was fairly slow or that its incorporation into the burial traditions and rites of the Picts was a gradual one. Dating from approximately the same time is a dressed slab with an incised cross from Temple. It would appear that, in Glenurquhart at least, therefore, Christianity had started to have a presence as the public expression of worship at sites like Temple, but that funerary rites and monuments were still regulated by older, non-Christian practices. Such a situation might be expected in the period of transition from a pantheistic to a monotheistic faith, where the new deity was accepted initially as part of the pantheon, with exclusivity only coming later.

The Great Glen was not the target of the missionaries. The monasteries that were founded in this period, such as Tarbat, Rosemarkie, Deer and Mortlach, were all reached through the Glen, but it received no major foundations of its own. However, it should be expected that this regular flow would have had an impact on Glen Mór. Each of the estates of the Glen is likely to have had an ecclesiastical centre, which at Urquhart would appear to have been the former pagan sanctuary at Temple. The cross slab from the site shows well Urquhart's position as a point on the communication route between Iona and the new establishments in the east of the country (**37**), bearing characteristics that are common to similar crosses on both sides of the

country. The cross is formed of incised lines describing its outline, but the 'armpits' of the cross are treated in a distinctive manner with small but well-defined hollows. This feature can be found on stones at the 7th-century foundation at Tullich in Aberdeenshire, as well as on Iona itself.

37 The cross slab from Temple

Late Pictish period

The history of the two centuries following the death of Bridei son of Mailcon can be read as a constant struggle for supremacy between the Scots, the Northumbrians, the Picts and the Britons of Strathclyde. The changing relationships form a complex quadrille, which was brought to a sudden end by the appearance of a new dance partner. The closing years of the 8th century saw the arrival of the Vikings. It is difficult to overstate the impact of the first devastating decades of Viking raiding. The carnage of the first attacks would be moderated in the following centuries by the settling of colonies occupying the islands to the north and west as well as Caithness and much of Sutherland. However, it was the warrior Vikings' destruction in battle of the key figures of the Pictish ruling dynasty that caused the chaos out of which the Dalriadan Cinaed mac Ailpín (Kenneth MacAlpin) emerged to take control of Pictland in the middle of the 9th century.

Few of these political changes seem to have made much impact on the Great Glen. It is not mentioned in records of the time and the only archaeological find that can be securely dated to this period is the fragment of a penanular brooch which was found somewhere in the vicinity of Urquhart (**38**). The brooch is very similar to several found in the St Ninian's Isle hoard from Shetland and has been dated to the late 8th century. However, as a stray find with no information regarding its context, it can tell us very little about Glen Mór at the time.

The one change that does appear to have made a difference is the realignment of the Pictish Church by King Nechtan, son of Derilei, in AD 710. He effectively broke the links with the Columban Church, allying Pictland with Northumbria and the mainstream of Europe, dampening the persistent influence of Dál Riata through Iona and introducing the hierarchical structure of the Roman Church as a useful bolster to secular control.

Nechtan's reforms are a clear example of the power of the Pictish kings, even if based in distant Fortriu, to dictate events across their kingdom. The church reforms he decreed were spearheaded by St Curitan, who took the name Boniface as a mark of his adherence to the Roman Church. St Curitan is an elusive figure, better known in legend than in history. He is especially associated with Rosemarkie where he established a church that in later centuries would become the cathedral of a new diocese. In the hills (*braes*) of Urquhart his name appears at a number of sites including *Clach Churadain*, the old chapel at Corrimony, and, at Buntait, *Croit Churadain* (Curitan's Croft) and *Tobar Churadain* (Curitan's Well). Local tradition held that Curitan and his companion, Gorman, were the first to preach in the Braes. Curitan is also commemorated at Struy in Strathglass and it is tempting to see the route of Curitan's mission from Rosemarkie entering the braes of Urquhart from the north. If there is any truth to the tradition that the Braes had been untouched by Christianity until the start of the 8th century, it would certainly add strength to the idea that the earlier missionaries from Iona had not seen the Great Glen and its tributaries as much more than a through-route.

The most visible manifestation of this newly reformed Church in Pictland was the monumental sculpture that it generated – the great cross slabs combining Christian and characteristically Pictish symbols. However, it is notable that within the Great Glen only a small fragment of decorated stone, from Dores, has any claim to

have come from a symbol-bearing cross slab. While one should always be cautious about drawing conclusions from an absence of evidence, the fact that the remarkable monuments, which were being erected around the Moray Firth in the 8th century, do not appear to have penetrated the Great Glen may be related to the absence of any major monastic foundation in the glen or, alternatively, to the loss or a weakening of Pictish cultural influence in the area.

38 Fragment of a silvered penanular brooch found near Urquhart, now in Inverness Museum and Art Gallery

Viking attacks and colonization

Viking attacks on sites in Britain started in the AD 790s, with the first recorded attack on Iona taking place in AD 795. The ferocity of these attacks is a matter of record and its impact was long-lasting, with the monks of Iona having to retreat to the comparative safety of Kells in Ireland and huge swathes of the north and west of Scotland becoming Norse territories. Viking raiding was focused, primarily, on centres of wealth such as monasteries, but nowhere within reach of the Norse longships could be considered safe. The records of Viking attacks in the Great Glen are derived entirely from local tradition. They are unreliable accounts but the existence of these legends is a mark of the impact the presence of the Vikings made in the area.

The first tradition concerns Inverlochy Castle, which is said to have been the location of a 'Pictish city' that was destroyed by the Vikings. Excavations in 1983 showed that the construction of the medieval castle disturbed earlier graves, but the suggestion of a Pictish city (whatever this might have meant) at this end of the Great Glen is clearly erroneous. A second legend of Viking raiding deals with an attack beyond the south-west end of the Glen, in the area around Crinan. In this tale Mony, the son of the king of Scandinavia, became separated from his ship and had to withdraw with his sister and a band of men up the Great Glen. Eventually they reached Glenurquhart where they made a brave stand on Craig Mony. Defeated, Mony and his sister escaped up Glenurquhart to Corrimony where Mony met his end, but his sister was spared and lived there for many years. It was believed in the 19th century that Craig Mony and Corrimony owed their names to this unfortunate raider, although they are more likely to be derived from the term *Monadh*, meaning a hill or hill-pasture. What these two traditions tell us is that for the inhabitants of the Great Glen, Viking raiding was not just something that happened somewhere else; whatever the actual levels of attacks in the Great Glen itself, the innate sense of threat was a real one.

While the image of Viking raiders is a persistent one, the greater impact of the Vikings seems to have come from the settlement of the north and west, which started early in the 9th century and established itself quickly. In the west they colonized the islands and much of the western seaboard, putting great pressure on the Scots of Dál Riata. In the north, the Jarldom of Orkney controlled Caithness and much of Sutherland and Easter Ross and, in its hunger for timber, stretched as far as the Beauly Firth. At the south-west end of the Great Glen the Cenél Loairn were struggling for their survival, while at the north-east end Glenurquhart was now bordering directly onto Norse territory along the River Beauly.

By the middle of the 9th century, the gradual takeover of Pictland by the kings of Dál Riata was firmly established under Cinaed mac Ailpín and his dynasty, with their territories on the western seaboard acting as a bulwark against the nascent Norse colonies. This eastward movement of Cenél nGabráin rulers into the south of Pictland appears to have been replicated by the Cenél Loairn, moving from Lorn and Morvern up the Great Glen to emerge as the rulers of Fidach, the province to be known from this point as Moray. This shift in the seat of Cenél Loairn influence may have happened as early as the late 8th century and may well have been made possible by intermarriage, producing a Cenél Loairn leader with a Pictish mother.

The mormaerdom of Moray

Between the 6th and 10th centuries, the Great Glen was transformed. It went from being a pagan land ruled by a Pictish high king whose rule stretched from Orkney to the Tay to being part of Christendom ruled by a regional, Scottish potentate, facing the constant threat of the expansion of its Norse neighbours. The cultural changes are reflected in the change of the province from the Pictish name of Fidach to the new name of Muréb or Moray, a change that may have been accompanied by a redrafting of the boundaries of the province. The political changes are marked by the new title of the rulers of the province; the position of sub-king or *regulus* is replaced by that of *mormaer*, or great steward. The appearance of the title at the start of the 10th century suggests a shift in the nature of kingship. Instead of the high king being the acknowledged foremost of the regional sub-kings, the redefinition of sub-king to steward indicates that the king's authority no longer stemmed from the consensus of the regional rulers but, conversely, they now relied on the king for the legitimation of their regional rule.

However, such constitutional technicalities are likely to have been diluted by distance, and it would appear that the position of mormaer of Moray was every bit as much as hereditary as that of *regulus* of Fidach, as the mormaerdom descended entirely through the branches of the Cenél Loairn. The autonomy of Moray was marked by Irish and Norse references to the Moray rulers as kings of the new, united kingdom of Alba. While chronicles always contain some inaccuracies, this was an error that appears to stem from the power and autonomy that the rulers of Moray enjoyed.

The independence of Moray was a mixed blessing, both for Moray and the kings of a unified Alba. Several mormaers died fighting the Norse earls of Orkney. It would appear that they were left to maintain Scotland's northern frontier while the kings interested themselves with the territories of Strathclyde and Lothian. However, while Moray provided a stout defence against the Norse, it was not an entirely subservient sentry. The Cenél Loairn, as mormaers of Moray, seem to have retained an element of rivalry with the Cenél nGabráin, as the MacAlpin kings of Alba, which may have resulted in the conflict which claimed the life of Cellach, mormaer of Moray in AD c.944 and King Dubh at Forres in AD 967. MacBeth was the only mormaer to have successfully challenged the MacAlpin line for the throne. Later chroniclers have painted him as a usurper and interloper, an aberration from the true line of succession from Cinaed mac Ailpín. The fictionalization of his story has added to the misinformation about one of the most interesting figures of the period.

MacBeth's father, Findlaech, had been murdered in c.1020 by his nephew Malcolm, who seized the mormaerdom. Malcolm was succeeded by his brother Gillecomgain who had married Gruoch, a granddaughter of either Cinaed II or Cinaed III, with whom he had a son, Lulach. In 1032, MacBeth recovered the mormaerdom by killing Gillecomgain and went on to marry Gruoch. When king Malcolm II died in 1034, the succession passed through his daughter to his grandson, Duncan, son of Crinan, lay-abbot of Dunkeld. For reasons that are not entirely clear, Duncan headed north to confront MacBeth in 1040 and was killed at Pitgaveny near

Elgin, either in battle or as an act of murder. It is possible that MacBeth's mother was, like Duncan's mother, a daughter of Malcolm II, but MacBeth's claim was enhanced by his wife Gruoch's claim, as a granddaughter of the royal line. While his 17-year reign was considered generally successful, he ultimately failed to establish a Cenél Loairn monarchy. Malcolm III (Canmore), the son of Duncan, succeeded in regaining the Crown for his family with Northumbrian backing. He destroyed MacBeth's fortress at Inverness before killing the man himself at Lumphanan in 1057. However, it is a mark of the strength of MacBeth's claim to the throne and the success of his reign that Malcolm was not accepted as king immediately. Lulach, MacBeth's stepson, appears to have been accepted as the second king of the house of Moray, but was killed in battle the following year at Essie, in Strathbogie.

While the Crown may have been lost to the house of Moray with the victory of Malcolm III at Essie, the mormaerdom remained with Lulach's son, Maelsnechtai. That this could happen is a mark of how much autonomy the mormaerdom had and how little influence a king such as Malcolm had as to who held this powerful position. However, Maelsnechtai was the third generation of mormaer to be defeated by Malcolm in 1078, retiring to a monastery to live out his days. With a rapid string of defeats against the Crown, the power of the mormaerdom was dwindling rapidly. In such a situation, it is a mark of the way in which chronicles were compiled that they become less detailed regarding individuals with less power. Maelsnechtai's son and heir as mormaer is thought to be Aedh (or Heth). Aedh is mentioned witnessing charters early in the 12th century, suggesting a reconciliation with the ruling house. He was succeeded in the mormaerdom by Angus – either Aedh's son or his nephew. In 1130 Angus staged an uprising against the Crown and was killed in battle at Stracathro.

The defeat at Stracathro represents the end of an era in Moray. The kings of Scotland would continue to struggle to control this area, which for many years to come would be the cradle of rebellions. However, the subsequent leaders of these rebellions were claimants to Moray or claimants to the Crown. When Angus died at Stracathro, he may well have been the last ruler of the north of Scotland who did not owe his position to the king in the south.

4

The first castle – Urquhart before the Wars of Independence

As early as the 17th century, the origins of the castle at Urquhart have been a matter of curiosity. In the 1650s, the eccentric Sir Thomas Urquhart of Cromarty wrote a history of his family entitled *Pantochronochanon: The true pedigree and lineal descent of the most antient and honourable family of the Urquharts*. His history writing was gargantuan in its ambitions and Munchausen-like in its achievement. We learn from Sir Thomas that he could trace his lineage all the way back to Adam and Eve, and that Urquhart Castle was founded by Beltistos Conachar in the year 554 BC. Like most of Sir Thomas's claims in this remarkable book, they are not to be trusted. However, the name of Conachar is one that appears not just in Sir Thomas's work but also in the histories of two other families, the Clan Forbes and the Clan MacKay, although details of each family's legends differ.

According to William MacKay, the 19th-century recorder of Glenurquhart's history and folklore, Conachar was an Irishman of the royal house of Ulster who fought on behalf of the king of Scotland in 1160 and was rewarded with Urquhart. He had three sons, William, the founder of Clan Urquhart, Alexander, the founder of Clan MacKay and John, the founder of Clan Forbes. Conachar does not appear in any historical documents that might confirm the truth of elements of these legends and remains for us a fabled figure, who, when hunting a boar which had already killed many people, was saved by the self-sacrifice of his aged but faithful great hound. He lived to a good age and was said to have been buried with his sword under Clach Ochonachair at Inchconachar, c. 4km (2½ miles) south-west of the castle.

39 David I and his grandson Malcolm IV (the Maiden)

Carving up Moray

With the death of Angus, mormaer of Moray, at Stracathro in 1130, David I took this opportunity to suppress the mormaerdom and seize its lands. As elsewhere in Scotland, the king started to allocate lands and estates to men he could trust in return for their strength of arms and loyalty. This new system of land tenure, known to us as feudalism, was one of David's lasting legacies and was extended by his grandsons, Malcolm IV (the Maiden) and William I (the Lion) (**39**). David I used the lands of Moray to plant the north with men of his own choosing. Foremost among them was Freskin, a Fleming who had already received lands in West Lothian before he was given the estate of Duffus, near Elgin.

This distribution of estates was done in two ways: thanage and fiefdom. A thane was an individual appointed to manage royal estates and to exercise judicial powers within the estate. Thanes were often minor landowners in their own right, holding the post for fairly short periods, with thanages rarely being hereditary. The thane was not an owner and was required to pay a set amount to the king each year, the estate's *cain*, as well as offering hospitality to the king if required, *conveth*. Fiefdom, in its purest form, was a grant of land in return for loyalty and military service. The grant of a fiefdom was generally hereditary although it had to be confirmed at each generation. The holders of a fiefdom were more important figures of society than thanes and may have held controlled military might. While fiefdom was an integral part of the new feudal system favoured by David I and his successors, thanage may have been related to earlier, Pictish forms of land tenure, and therefore simpler to introduce in former Pictish territory. Thanages also had one further advantage for the king: because the tribute from a thanage was paid in produce rather than military service, they helped ensure the financial stability of the Crown's coffers.

David seems to have been cautious about biting off more of the vast territories of Moray than he could chew. Inverness seems to have been the limit of the fiefdoms in his reign, with any further stretch of royal control being under thanages. These do not appear in the records as frequently as the fiefdoms, as they were often held by figures who were not as important and who were unlikely to be outsiders to the region.

Conachar would have been a suitable candidate for a thanage as a trusted but not particularly influential figure. We know that both Malcolm IV and William I were active in extending the settlement of Moray as part of their attempts to exercise greater control there. William is said to have '*moved the Moray-men*' in 1163, possibly a reference to the replacement of local leaders with men of his own choosing, and in 1179 he established new royal castles at Edirdour (Redcastle on the south coast of the Black Isle) and Dunskeath (at the mouth of the Cromarty Firth). While we may never know whether Conachar should be considered to be part of history or part of legend, the installation of a trusted figure into a thanage of Urquhart would be entirely consistent with the other events of the later 12th century. Indeed, it might explain why none of Conachar's three sons are said to have inherited land which he held as an official rather than as an owner.

The mac Heths and the mac Williams

Extending royal control over Moray in the 12th and 13th centuries was not a simple matter. Even with the mormaerdom suppressed, Moray was not used to being truly ruled by Scotland south of the Mounth and resistance was galvanized by the descendants of Lulach.

When Angus of Moray fell at Stracathro in 1130 his ally, Malcolm mac Heth, escaped and fought on. Much ink has been spilt discussing the identity of Malcolm mac Heth. When he was captured in 1134, he was not killed; instead he was held at Roxburgh, remaining a prisoner until his release in 1157, at which point he was granted the earldom of Ross. It has been suggested that the reluctance to despatch mac Heth suggests that he was closely related to the king, possibly the illegitimate son of Alexander I and grandson of Malcolm III. However, his patronimic, mac Heth, suggests that he was descended from Aedh (or Heth), mormaer of Moray early in David's reign. The matter is further confused by the curious figure of Wimund, bishop of Argyll. In 1142, while Malcolm mac Heth was incarcerated at Roxburgh, Wimund staged a rebellion, claiming to be the son of the mormaer of Moray. He suffered for his pretension, living out his days, mutilated, in the monastery of Byland. The relationships between Aedh, Angus, Malcolm and Wimund are not understood, although they could all easily be close relatives pressing successive claims rather than rivals for the mormaerdom.

The mac Heth line was not without allies, and in 1156 Somerled, lord of Argyll, rose in rebellion against Malcolm IV, supported by his nephews, the sons of Malcolm mac Heth, and it would appear that the release of Malcolm in 1157 was an attempt to pacify this resistance. Indeed the earldom of Ross, granted to Malcolm mac Heth, may represent the northern half of the mormaerdom of Moray, effectively giving mac Heth some of the lands he sought.

One characteristic of this struggle in the 12th century is the evidence of continued links between the mormaerdom of Moray and the western seaboard. Not only did mac Heth marry a sister of Somerled of Argyll, the apparent appointment of a member of the house of Moray to the bishopric of the Isles can only have taken place with the consent of secular powers in the west. It would appear that the Great Glen was still providing a direct link between Moray and Argyll, bypassing the heart of royal control.

The mac Heth threat did not evaporate with the granting of the earldom of Ross to Malcolm and, indeed, it was made more dangerous by the merging of the mac Heth claims to Moray with claims to the throne itself. Donald mac William was the grandson of an illegitimate child of Duncan II. His sister had married Harald Maddadson, earl of Orkney, and his mother had been the daughter of Aedh, mormaer of Moray, thereby inheriting a mac Heth claim as well. Such a pedigree was too impressive to be ignored, but not strong enough to prosper. With Harald's support, Donald rebelled in 1181, and for the next six years he caused trouble in Ross and Moray including taking the royal castle of Auldearn. He was eventually defeated at Inverness by forces loyal to William the Lion.

Further mac William/mac Heth rebellions took place in 1211–12, 1215 and

40 Duffus Castle. The masonry structures are replaced timber elements of the first motte-and-bailey castle

1228–29. We have few details about the events of these risings other than the occasional mention of the loss of a royal castle to the rebels; Redcastle or Dunskeath followed Auldearn in falling to the rebels in 1211. However, the disruption to life in Ross and Moray appears to have been pervasive, such that in 1215 special papal protection was extended from Rome over several churches that had been ransacked in recent troubles. One of the churches named in this is Kilmore, *'the church of Urquhart beyond Inverness'*. The mac William/mac Heth saga ended in savagery, with the authorized public murder of an infant girl at the market cross in Forfar in 1230. The mac William/mac Heth cause had been a major threat to peace and stability in the north for a very long time, this infant was the last of the line and these were brutal times.

Feudalism in the Glen

The form of any 12th-century fortification at Urquhart is a matter of speculation. The 12th century saw the arrival in Moray of the motte-and-bailey castle. A castle of this form, such as Duffus, built on lands given to Freskin the Fleming, lord of Strathbrock by David I, did not rely on a rocky eminence for its defences but rather gained much of its impact from rising out of flat ground. The distribution of mottes across the north of Scotland is largely restricted to the east of the country and is associated, if not with incoming magnates, then with those who were adopting the system of fiefdoms. The east of the country was the area of greatest penetration of feudalism and the new nobility in the 12th and 13th centuries, and the motte was both a new form of defence and a very visible symbol of the new order.

That the 12th-century kings did make some inroads into the Glen is shown by another element of their reforms – the Church. David I is credited with the establishment of the parochial system in Scotland. In the south of Scotland, this was closely bound to the establishment of fiefdoms, as the recipient of the estate was required to build a church that would, subsequently, receive the teinds (or tithes) of the estate. Parishes therefore developed in parallel with the division of estates. By the opening years of the 13th century we learn not only that the church of Kilmore had already been established as the parochial church of Urquhart but that the teinds from the church were to be diverted to support the chancellor of the diocese of Moray. For the parish to become established it is likely that the estate would need to exist as a thanage or fiefdom, giving further support to Urquhart being granted to a figure such as Conachar.

The earliest reference we have to an outsider being granted land in the Great Glen is a charter associated with the creation of a parish. In 1225, Thomas of Thirlestane, from Lauderdale in the Borders, granted a croft and toft (a manse and glebe) to the rector of the parish of Abertarff. This would appear to mark the establishment of a new parish, echoing the grant of Abertarff as a new fiefdom. However Thomas's tenure at the south end of Loch Ness was to be brief; in 1228 he was killed when his timber castle was attacked and burnt by Gillescop mac William. The timber castle was a motte, and, like Duffus (**40**), it rose from relatively flat ground rather than occupying a rocky knoll. The last traces of the motte were destroyed when Fort Augustus was built on its site, but 18th-century records indicate that the motte was formed at the edge of an alluvial terrace 2.5m (8ft) high by cutting a ditch to separate the motte from the rest of the flat ground (**41**).

41 Abertarff Motte, the "Old Castle of Kiliwhiman", recorded by the Board of Ordnance in 1718 before the site was cleared to make way for Fort Augustus

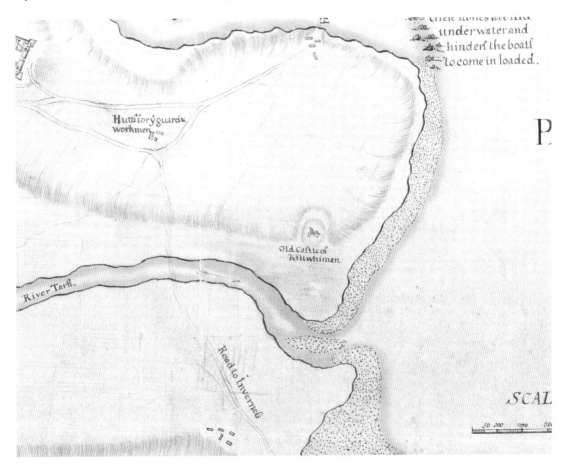

The new masters of Moray

It is not known when Thomas received a grant of land at Abertarff. It is possible that he had not been installed in his motte for long when the last mac William/mac Heth rebellion swept up the Great Glen before burning Inverness. It was the suppression of the rebellions of the early 13th century that brought to the fore the families who were to shape Moray until the Wars of Independence. When Guthred mac William rose in rebellion in 1211, the post of justiciar of Scotia was held by William Comyn. In this role, he led an army of 4,000 against Guthred, assisted by the earl of Atholl, and the two claimants to the earldom of Mar – Malcolm, son of Morgrund, and Thomas Durward. In 1212, Comyn's reward for success was being entrusted with the hand of Marjorie, daughter of Fergus, earl of Buchan and the lands that went with the title. In 1229, after the suppression of the final mac William rising under Gillescop, the Comyn family was rewarded with the lordship of Badenoch, which included Lochaber.

If the Comyn family prospered from their service to the Crown, the Durwards also did well, if not quite so well. Like the Comyns, the Durwards had made their name at the Scottish court in the 13th century, earning the hereditary post of the king's door ward, hence the sobriquet, Durward. Another feature the Durwards shared with the Comyns was their ambition. Thomas Durward, eager to reach the highest levels of a stratified knightly court, capitalized on the favour earned in defeating the king's enemies to press his claim to the earldom of Mar. The suit failed but he was compensated with extensive estates centred on Coull and Lumphanan in Deeside, lands apparently sliced out of the lands of Mar. Durward was also made sheriff of Inverness; his son Alan was given the estate of Urquhart and another relative, Gilbert, received Boleskine on the south side of Loch Ness.

The Durwards and the Comyns were not the only families who were granted estates in return for services rendered. After 1229, the death of Thomas of Thirlestane left the estate of Abertarff in need of a new lord, and it was granted to William Bisset. John Bisset already had the extensive lordship of the Aird at the head of the Beauly Firth and to the north of Glenurquhart, and Walter Bisset was given the lands of Stratherrick to the south-east of Loch Ness. Therefore, almost the entire periphery of Loch Ness seems to have been held by two families, the Durwards and the Bissets.

Along with the Comyns, the Bissets and the Durwards were part of the wave of rising families who prospered under the Canmore kings. The Bissets, Norman in origin, had come to Scotland seeing opportunities for advancement, while the Durwards, descended from an Angus family, were a good example of an indigenous family who had profited by assuming the new attitudes and practices of the Canmore courts. However, to the inhabitants of the Great Glen, both families were considered outsiders and their acquisition of the north-east half of the Glen must have been a dramatic change.

The production of charters and other documents was a by-product of the new feudal system and, as a result, the documentary record is skewed in favour of this aspect of Scottish history and culture. For the lands beyond Abertarff we have no records of any owners before the lordships of Badenoch and Lochaber were given to the Comyn family. However, the fact that Gillescop mac William's rising seems to have originated at the south-west end of the Glen, moving up it to destroy Abertarff and Inverness, raises the possibility that the mac Williams had been the previous owners of the Comyns' new Lochaber lands.

Durward's Urquhart

When Alan Durward took possession of Urquhart, probably some time around 1230, he was taking on lands that appear to have been harried by the recent uprisings. The existence of the parish church suggests that Alan's predecessor at Urquhart had made headway in bringing the government of Urquhart and Glenmoriston into line with the rest of Scotland under Alexander II's control. In the absence of any evidence for a motte similar to Abertarff, it seems probable that the site of the Pictish fort on Strone Point, almost certainly still visible in the 12th century, had been reoccupied. The most dramatic mottes of 12th-century Scotland rose out of flat ground, but the site of Urquhart Castle, with its high boss and lower, wider terraces, lent itself to easy adaptation of the motte-and-bailey model with far less investment.

Alan Durward set about making Urquhart a stronghold fitting for the great potentate that he aspired to be. The most radical change that he made was the cutting of the great ditch through solid rock. This new ditch transformed the site from being a rocky knoll with defensive potential to a major fortification, capable of withstanding a concerted attack. The ditch at Urquhart has never been accurately dated by archaeologists. However, it bears close comparison with fortifications at one of the Durward family's other castles. At Coull, on Deeside, the ditch is of a similar scale to that at Urquhart and, as at Urquhart, it cuts the castle off from the gently rising slope (**42**). The ditches at both castles are characterized by a counter-scarp bank on the outside edge of the ditch and a shallow terrace between the ditch and the castle walls.

As with mottes elsewhere that were being upgraded, Durward kept the essential structure of the motte and bailey, but strengthened it in stone. The highest point of the site now housed a small citadel enclosed by the masonry

42 Coull Castle, Aberdeenshire

of a shell keep. The lower areas, which were probably protected by a palisade, housed the hall, workshops, kitchens, stabling and all the other accommodation needed for a military base that wished to be taken seriously. The area enclosed by Durward's castle made it one of the largest in Scotland. It is not clear how much this was a reflection of the perceived military need and how much Durward's aspirations.

A castle as large as Urquhart represented a very major settlement in 13th-century Scotland. Most of the population lived in scattered rural settlements, which would not coalesce beyond the size of townships until the 18th century. As well as being a military base, Urquhart, like every feudal seat, was the civic centre of the estate; it was the focus for tax collection, the source of protection and the arena of justice. Taxes were paid in kind and large parts of the castle were set aside for the storage of produce, either for consumption later in the year, or for shipment on to Durward's other residences, to markets or to royal stores. However, the inhabitants of the castle needed to eat as well, and part of the estate was set aside for providing food for the castle's table. As with most castles, the farm closest to Urquhart fulfilled this function and its name, Borlum (a corruption of Board Land), reflects this role: it was the land that provided the food for the board, or table. The Great Glen has two other Borlums; one not far from the site of Abertarff motte at Fort Augustus and the other to the south-west of Inverness, probably serving the motte at Holm House.

With Alan Durward's death in 1275, his property was divided between his three daughters. However, Urquhart seems to have reverted to the Crown and to have been swiftly granted to the Comyn family, further strengthening their hold over the north of Scotland. Like a new homeowner, the Comyns seem to have made improvements to Alan Durward's fortress. While Durward had retained the southern summit as the focus for his castle, the Comyns seem to have built up the rest of the site to create a more imposing residence. A new tower was created at the north end of the site, presumably for the most prestigious accommodation. A new, stone-built great hall was constructed overlooking the lochside, which was now protected by a wall following the line of the rock. The landward access was now controlled by a grand gatehouse sporting a pair of drum towers, rapidly joined by a masonry curtain taking the place of Durward's palisade. The 13th century in Scotland has been described as the golden age of castles, and the recasting of Urquhart, with its major defences and buildings built in masonry, can be seen as part of this wider movement. The mottes favoured in the previous century were impressive and relatively quick to build, but masonry construction, although requiring far greater investment, produced buildings of far greater strength and permanence.

Changes in the Great Glen

Alan Durward, the Comyns and the unfortunate Thomas of Thirlestane were not the only castle builders in the Great Glen (**43**). The most important and oldest castle in the Glen was at Inverness. It was first constructed by Malcolm III Canmore, after he had destroyed MacBeth's castle nearby in the middle of the 11th century. It was

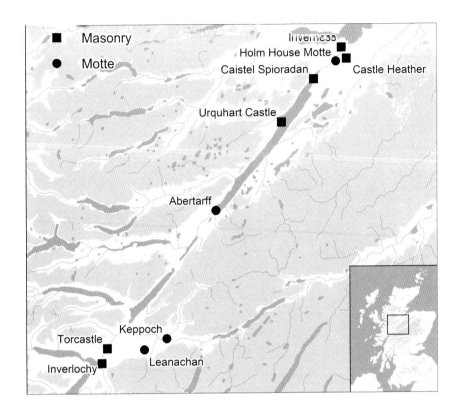

43 *Mottes and masonry castles in the Great Glen*

probably refortified as part of David I's construction of a chain of royal castles along the south side of the Moray Firth. Later redevelopment of the castle site has made it impossible to be sure of the form of David's castle, other than it was almost certainly a variation on the standard motte and bailey being constructed elsewhere.

In addition to a chain of royal castles across the Laigh of Moray, in the second half of the 12th century, burghs were established adjacent to and under the protection of each royal motte. Economic development was the third element of the reforms of the 12th century, and the creation of burghs with protected trading rights was an effective way of encouraging commerce. The development of Inverness as a trading centre created a new focal point at this end of the Glen. When Gillescop mac William burnt the motte at Abertarff and the burgh of Inverness in 1228, he was attacking two foundations that had been brought into the area by outsiders. Inverness became the trading port for much of the Highlands, but its contact with the wider world resulted in distinctions arising between Inverness and its hinterland. Foremost among these was the language, with Gaelic having a far weaker hold in the trading burgh than it had in the valleys and glens away from the coast.

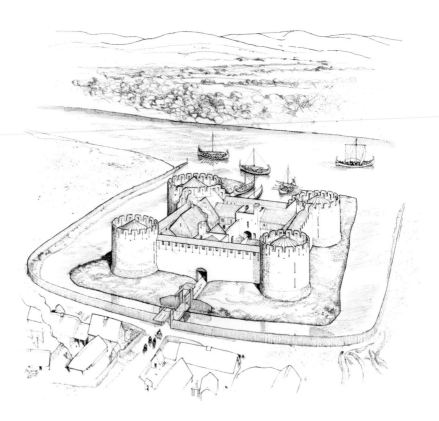

44 *Inverlochy Castle*
with the River
Lochy behind

Inverness and Urquhart were both in the Moray half of the Great Glen. The western half of the Glen, the former territory of Dál Riata, now opened on to the realm of Somerled and his heirs. Somerled has been seen as a key character in the history of western Scotland; he was both Norse and Scottish, the lord of the Isles and the embodiment of a man of Argyll. He rebelled against two kings, of Norway and Scotland respectively, to create a domain of his own. An important characteristic of this domain was its marine nature – it would be misleading to think of it as a territory; its focus was the sea and the most important locations were, essentially, those that were important for a maritime society. For this reason the Great Glen was a long way from the centre of things for the lords of the Isles.

When Gillescop's rebellion was defeated in 1229, one of the rewards the Comyns had received was the lordship of Badenoch, which brought with it not just the upper Spey valley but also Lochaber. The Comyns now had territory that ran, almost unbroken, from one side of the country to the other. Their principal line of communication though was not through the Great Glen, but through their own territories in Strathspey and Glen Spean. A base was needed for such operations and work started on a new castle at Inverlochy around 1260, judging from the architectural style of the building (**44**). The dating of the construction of Inverlochy is of interest in itself. The Comyns had been granted Lochaber a generation before, in 1230, but started building Inverlochy at a time when the Norwegian hold on the western seaboard was, finally, being loosened, and relationships were being forged with the MacDougall family, that branch of Somerled's offspring which controlled lower Loch Linnhe. Marriage between Alexander MacDougall, the fourth chief of the clan, and the daughter of John Comyn, earl of Buchan, cemented an allegiance that must have made the job of the lord of Lochaber very much easier.

While the form of Urquhart had been influenced by the existing topography and previous structures, Inverlochy, an entirely new castle, borrowed the latest ideas of castle design from the Welsh Marches and the Crusaders in the Holy Land. Inverlochy, more than any Highland castle before it, was an architectural expression of strength and order. A square plan with a round tower on each corner, the large courtyard in the middle would have been filled with timber buildings; a hard shell with a soft centre. Around the outside of this castle the Comyns dug a moat, fed with water from the adjacent river Lochy.

The Comyns were probably also responsible for the appearance of mottes at the mouth of Glen Spean, the route between their castles of Inverlochy in Lochaber and Ruthven in Badenoch. While mottes may have fallen from favour as the preferred form of a noble's castle, they were still a useful form for small staging posts in potentially hostile country. It is possible that the mottes at Keppoch near Roy Bridge and Leanachan at the foot of Aonach Mór served this purpose.

The Church in the Glen

While the new castles built in the 12th and 13th centuries were a dramatic addition to the landscape of the Great Glen, they were few and far between. A more pervasive change in this period is likely to have been the way in which religious life was ordered. The creation of the parishes of the Great Glen, almost certainly based on estate boundaries, identified a single church in each parish as the main church.

45 Probable medieval church and chapel sites in Glenurquhart

However, while such an arrangement might work in a small, lowland parish, the scale of a parish such as Urquhart and Glenmoriston meant that a single church could not be expected to serve people who lived so far away. Before these parochial reforms there were a large number of chapels and holy sites across a parish. In Glenurquhart alone there was Kilmore (adopted as the parish church), St Ninians at Temple, Kilmichael, Lag ant-Seapail and Achnahannet near Bunloit, St Curitan's Church at Corrimony, a possible chapel at Pitkerrald and, no doubt, other sites now lost to us (**45**).

While the new institution of the parish had little use for these places, the

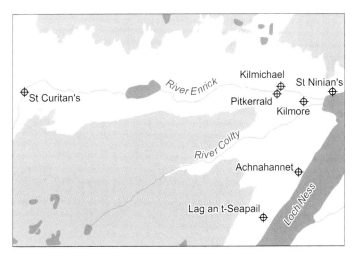

*46 Beauly Priory one
of a very small number
of medieval monasteries
in the Highlands*

population of a parish as large as Urquhart and Glenmoriston could not be served without them. Sites such as St Curitan's survived as subsidiary chapels and local cemeteries serving the immediate neighbourhood. St Ninians, the church at Temple, survived through specializing – it appears to have been the oldest ecclesiastical site in Glenurquhart, housed a relic of St Drostan and was adjacent to a venerated well and trees. By acting as a local shrine, St Ninians survived and even prospered as the largest church in the parish other than Kilmore. For the other sites, if they had chapel buildings at all, they would have been very modest affairs, since parishes such as Urquhart, with their teinds being allocated to a distant official such as the chancellor of Moray, found it notoriously difficult even to maintain the parish church.

The boundary between the reformed dioceses of Moray and Argyll reflected the split between the eastern and western halves of the Glen and, probably, helped reinforce this distinction. The other element of church reforms at the time, the reformed monastic orders, are notably absent from the Great Glen. The Bissets did succeed in establishing the only monastery in the area, Beauly Priory, a Valliscaulian house, in c.1230 (**46**). This was joined by a Dominican friary in Inverness, founded by Alexander II. The Highlands in general were not particularly appealing to the monastic orders, however, which favoured areas where sizeable endowments of productive lands were available.

Trade and timber

The final innovation in this period, the creation of burghs, will have also had an impact on life in the Great Glen. Inverness was now the official forum in which trade was to take place. This was a mixed blessing for the population in that it made taxation easier to impose but also brought producers and buyers together more easily. Timber remained an important export out of Inverness and Glenurquhart, with its easy transport by water, was in a good position to supply it. Across Europe, agricultural expansion was making good quality timber a prized commodity as woodlands made way for agriculture. This in its turn also seems to have given Inverness something of a reputation for shipbuilding. Matthew Paris, the English chronicler, records that in 1249 a Frenchman, Hugh, count of St Paul and Blois, had a wonderful ship made in Inverness to take him on crusade to the Holy Land.

The Wars of Independence

The Wars of Independence have, too often, been portrayed as a simple struggle between Scotland and England, glossing over those aspects of the conflict that would otherwise be considered to arise from civil war (**47**). In simplistic terms, the Wars of Independence can be seen as having three protagonists: England, pursuing the expansionist policies of Edward I; the Balliol cause, striving to retain Scotland as it had been under Alexander III; and the Bruce cause, advancing the Bruce family's rival claim to the Crown. The Balliol cause was dominated by the power and influence of the Comyn family. They had much to lose and, as a result, decisions such as the submission to Edward in 1296 and 1304 seem to have been pragmatic ones, aimed at retaining life, lands and influence. Championed by William Wallace, the Balliol cause was the focus of Scottish resistance until it became clear that John Balliol was not going to return from his estates in France and Robert the Bruce provided an alternative in his rising against Edward in 1306. Bruce's rising was a blow to the weakened Balliol/Comyn circle and a cutting loose from his own English allegiances. It is only after this that Robert the Bruce became the lodestone to Scottish resistance, earning his unassailable place in Scottish history.

47 *Penny from the reign of King Edward I of England found at Urquhart*

The crisis of succession that followed the death of the Maid of Norway, granddaughter of Alexander III, in 1290 for a time seems to have affected the north very little. The selection of John Balliol as king in 1292 supported the status quo of Comyn supremacy in the area: Balliol's sister was the wife of John Comyn of Badenoch. However, when war broke out in 1296 its impact was felt rapidly across the country. Edward I's invasion was swift and sweeping – sacking Berwick in March, crushing a Scottish force at Dunbar in April, accepting Balliol's abdication at the start of July and reaching Elgin by the end of the same month. From Elgin he sent out sorties to Badenoch, the heart of the territory of the senior branch of the Comyn family, and other regions beyond the Laigh of Moray.

The impact on life in the Great Glen was twofold: not only did the war come to the north but the men of the north fought far from home. Following the sack of Berwick, William, earl of Ross, along with the earls of Menteith and Atholl, carried out a revenge attack on Tynedale and Redesdale. The earl of Ross was again in the field at the Battle of Dunbar when, among the Scottish prisoners taken were John of Glenurquhart and Christine of the Aird, the son of one of the earl's vassals, John of the Aird. The fact that these two are mentioned by name in the records suggests that they were men of some standing. They had followed their feudal lord to war and it is likely that they brought with them men from their own lands.

While Scotland, in the midst of invasion in 1296, had capitulated to Edward, the reaction came the following year. William Wallace led a rising in the south, which was complemented by Andrew de Moray in the north, Duncan MacDougall in the west and James Stewart and Robert the Bruce in the south-west. Andrew de Moray's rising was the first. He gathered a force, including a number of Inverness burgesses, at his castle of Avoch (Ormond) on the Black Isle. The English were aware of his activities and summoned the constable of Urquhart, William fitz Warine, to Inverness on Sunday, 26 May to discuss the situation. On the way back to Urquhart at the end of the day, fitz Warine was attacked by de Moray and his men. The skirmish was clearly quite a substantial encounter, with fitz Warine losing two men and 18 horses. The following day de Moray and his troops besieged fitz Warine in Urquhart Castle. However, fitz Warine was not without support. The countess of Ross sent him a messenger offering her help and explaining that she had no part in de Moray's hostility. He turned down her offer but she then sent her son with supplies to provision the castle. The actions of the countess appear to have been largely governed by the fact that her husband was a prisoner of the English.

48 *Penny from the reign of King John Balliol found at Urquhart*

During the night of the 27th, de Moray staged an attack, killing several of the defenders including fitz Warine's son, Richard. The tactic of a night attack was the most sensible option for a lightly equipped force and it comes as little surprise that the siege did not persist. Possibly as a reaction to the intervention of the countess of Ross and John of the Aird (whose son was being held at Corffe Castle in Dorset), de Moray raised the siege and retreated to Avoch and the neighbouring woods. With such rebels at large, on 11 June Edward I ordered the bishop of Aberdeen and Gartnait, the son of the earl of Mar

> *... to proceed to the foresaid castle [Urquhart] without any delay, and see the condition of it; and thereafter, in consultation with the said William [fitz Warine], provide and direct that the castle may be so strengthened and garrisoned that no damage or danger may in any way occur to it.*

It is not clear whether they ever got as far as Urquhart. Shortly after this date fitz Warine was appointed as the new constable of Stirling Castle, and it is possible that he managed to effect a dignified retreat from the Great Glen which preserved his life and liberty. By mid July de Moray had moved out from his base on the Black Isle to secure Urquhart, Inverness, Banff, Elgin and Aberdeen, appointing Sir Alexander Forbes to hold Urquhart in the name of John Balliol (**48**).

At the other end of the Great Glen, Duncan MacDougall, son of Alexander

MacDougall of Argyll, was fighting a campaign against the MacDonalds of Islay, whom Edward had appointed bailie of Argyll and the Isles. While Andrew de Moray was securing the Comyn lands in the north-east of the country, MacDougall based himself at the Comyn castle of Inverlochy, using two great galleys in his campaign against the MacDonalds. Edward I's reaction to this rising suggests that he understood it as being fuelled by the resentment of having outsiders controlling these territories. He released Alexander MacDougall of Argyll, John Comyn, lord of Badenoch and John Comyn, earl of Buchan with instructions to bring their hereditary territories to order. Needless to say, these men were deliberately ineffective in reining in their relatives. While the rising of 1297 did not succeed in driving English forces out of Scotland completely, for the next six years the north was largely free of English interference and functioned as a truncated nation under the Guardians of Scotland; Parliament sat, courts were held, sheriffs were appointed and officials were paid.

War continued in the south of Scotland, but, with Edward fighting wars on the Continent at the same time, his forces were stretched and made little advance beyond the Forth. However, treaty with France in May 1303 brought Edward's attention rapidly back to Scotland. Mimicking his campaign of 1296, he penetrated deep into Scotland, sweeping up the east coast, through Buchan and on to install himself at John Comyn of Badenoch's island stronghold of Lochindorb. This destination betrays a key part of Edward's motivation in planning the route of his campaign. For the six years since Andrew de Moray's rising the north of Scotland had been out of English control and Comyn had been orchestrating the government of Scotland. The occupation of Comyn's inaccessible Lochindorb was the symbolic act that proclaimed Edward's domination of that part of Scotland which had remained beyond his grasp.

As in 1296, Urquhart was attacked by English forces. Sir Andrew Forbes was still the constable of Urquhart in 1303 and while other castles such at Inverness fell with little resistance, Forbes's stand was little short of heroic. Besieged, and having exhausted the garrison's provisions, Forbes sent his pregnant wife through enemy lines to safety before he and his garrison staged a desperate counterattack on the besiegers camped on the slope opposite the castle. It was a valiant act, worthy of this age of chivalry, but, weakened and outnumbered, the Scottish garrison fell.

In 1305 the Comyns, the stalwarts of the Guardianship, came to an accommodation with England, while Robert the Bruce, who had assisted in Edward's 1303 invasion, became increasingly alienated from the English. Matters came to a head in early February 1306, when Bruce stumbled into rebellion by murdering John Comyn of Badenoch in the church of the Greyfriars in Dumfries. It would appear that this was not a premeditated act but rather the result of an impetuous argument. However, by killing the leading figure of Scottish politics, Bruce had effectively launched a coup.

By the end of March 1306 he had achieved a string of military successes across south-west Scotland and was made king at Scone, supported by a new faction who were not united by Comyn allegiances. Bruce's surprise rebellion was brought to a shuddering halt by the English victory at Methven in June. Bruce went on the run until the following spring, preparing his next move among friends in Argyll and the Islands. His campaign of 1307 started in his home territories of Carrick before building momentum and moving further afield. The death of Edward I in July took the vigour out of the English opposition and Bruce focused his attack on the Comyns and their allies.

In November 1307 he took an army across Rannoch Moor to seize Inverlochy, before moving up the Great Glen to take Urquhart and Inverness. This gave him a strong base that strategically split two of his key enemies: the Comyns to the east and the earl of Ross to the north. In 1304 Urquhart had been described to Edward I as one of the strongest fortresses in the country. It would have offered Bruce a secure garrison in potentially hostile territory, especially having secured the Great Glen behind him. The following months saw Bruce obtain control of north-east Scotland, devastating Buchan as he did so, and force the earl of Ross into a truce, which was converted to an oath of loyalty the following year.

The wars against England continued for many years to come but, having secured the north and greatly curtailed the power of the Comyns, Bruce's attention was focused in later years on the west, where the MacDougalls persisted in causing problems for the new king, and the south, where the English were more difficult to dislodge. Urquhart, removed from Comyn custody, became a royal castle, while the new power in the north was to be Bruce's trusted nephew, Thomas Randolph, the first holder of the newly created earldom of Moray.

Urquhart's role in the struggle is worth investigation. There are several points worth bearing in mind when considering this. Urquhart was rarely at the centre of the struggles in the Wars of Independence, with the greatest battles taking place in the south of Scotland. However, while the Scottish Guardianship retained control of the north, it could not be destroyed by the English. Similarly, if Bruce was to be successful in ensuring the acceptance of his young reign, he could not permit the north to remain out of his control. Urquhart Castle was important in the control of the north not so much because of its position (Inverness was by far the more important location strategically) but because of its size and strength. Admittedly, very little can move on Loch Ness without coming to the attention of those at Urquhart, but the various armies seem to have used the Great Glen very little before Bruce's campaign of 1307. However, any force seeking to control the north could not permit a castle of the stature of Urquhart to remain out of its control. The fortress created by Alan Durward and the Comyns, with its mighty ditch and masonry walls, was recognized as being one of the strongest castles in the land and could act as a reservoir for constant insurgency if left in the hands of the enemy.

5

The later castle –
Urquhart under attack

The Highlands have had a notoriously turbulent history, and the 14th and 15th centuries have a better claim than most to being a period of particular turmoil. The re-emergence of wars with England in the middle of the 14th century, the deliberate destruction and disorder caused by Alexander Stewart, earl of Buchan (the 'Wolf of Badenoch') in the 1380s and 1390s and the attempts to expand MacDonald control until the end of the 15th century, all contributed to the disruption of civil life and the continued weakness of royal control. However, from this crucible emerged what are now well-known clans, such as the Camerons, the Grants, the Frasers and the numerous branches of the Clan Donald, as those wielding power locally exploited the commotions of the time to advance their own interests and protect their supporters. This period has a special place in Highland history, defining the patterns of kinship and loyalty that were the foundations of the social structure of the Great Glen for the next 300 years, and which still underpin how the Highlands are viewed and Highlanders view themselves.

The constables

Following Robert the Bruce's capture of Urquhart Castle in 1307 it never again fell into English hands. In about 1312, the castle and barony of Urquhart were among the many honours that the king showered on his nephew, Thomas Randolph, the new earl of Moray. Randolph had lands throughout Scotland but, by granting him many of the former Comyn territories in the north, the king placed Randolph in a vice-regal role north of the Mounth. His role in governing the north was, essentially, the same as that which the Comyns had played on behalf of Alexander III and John Balliol; it was a pattern of government that had been highly effective and which Robert I sought to repeat. Randolph's political position during the reign of Robert I (and as Guardian after the king's death in 1329) made Urquhart a royal castle in all but name. Indeed in 1332, when Randolph was acting as Guardian for the young David II, it was the Royal Exchequer that paid for the provisioning of the castle.

Urquhart was one of many strongholds that Thomas Randolph held. The possession of such castles carried with it obligations to fortify, garrison and provision them for the service of the Crown and the defence of the nation. The practicalities of such a duty were not a matter to concern such a great magnate, and a constable was appointed to fulfil these obligations. Throughout the 14th century the constable was a particularly important position at Urquhart, changing less frequently than the ownership. While the owners were likely to have had some impact at Urquhart –

possibly instigating some of the major building works, such as the expansion of the buildings around the great hall – the constable of Urquhart seems to have taken on much of the role normally associated with the owner. The position of constable in a medieval castle was, essentially, a military one, and therefore differed from the role of the steward, who was expected to manage the estate and household in his lord's absence. However, at Urquhart we have many references to the constable in this period but none at all to a steward, which suggests that here the two roles may have been combined.

The first constable we have on record under the Randolph earls of Moray is Sir Robert Lauder of Quarrelwood. Although his own estate of Quarrelwood was just outside Elgin, he hailed from the same part of the Borders as Sir Thomas of Thirlestane a century before. While the Lauders were not of the rank of great magnates, Sir Robert was clearly a man of substance. He seems to have taken lands in the north as a vassal and supporter of Thomas Randolph and was made justiciar of the north in 1328. Lauder appears to have been a valued member of the Randolph circle, for which he and his family were rewarded. In 1345 Lauder's grandson, Sir Robert Chisholm, received land in Glenurquhart and at Invermoriston from John, third earl of Moray, and the following year Chisholm was fighting alongside the earl at the Battle of Neville's Cross.

It was Sir Robert Lauder who, in 1334, was responsible for the stout resistance of the English siege that followed Edward Balliol's invasion of Scotland. At this stage, Urquhart was one of only five castles to remain in Scottish hands. The provisions paid for by the Exchequer in 1332 may well have been invaluable in a lengthy siege, but they are unlikely to be the only item of expenditure the Crown made on Urquhart. Having endured the English siege, Lauder remained as constable for the next 25 years. His success in resisting English aggression did his status no harm whatsoever, and he was appointed one of the commissioners for the peace treaty with England in 1335.

When the barony of Urquhart reverted to the Crown with the death of the third earl of Moray at Neville's Cross in 1346, Lauder remained as constable. Indeed, for all intents and purposes, it is likely that there was little perceptible change in the running of the castle and the estate following the earl's death; Sir Robert Lauder was still in charge. As early as 1334 he had strengthened his personal connections with Glenurquhart by obtaining for himself grants of lands at Abriachan and Achmony from the bishop of Moray. In 1342 it was he, rather than the earl of Moray, who hosted at Urquhart the signing of a charter by William, earl of Ross granting the lands of Kintail to Ranald MacRuairi, brother-in-law to John of the Isles, witnessed by the bishops of Ross and Moray.

In 1363, four years after he resigned the post of constable, Sir Robert received a pension from the king, which doubtless helped offset his expenditure from the previous year in founding a chaplainry at Elgin Cathedral. However, perhaps the clearest mark of Lauder's success as constable of Urquhart was not his pension or his longevity in the position but that his successor was his own grandson, Sir Robert Chisholm. While the Chisholm family, like the Lauders, came from the Borders, it was under Sir Robert Chisholm that they became established as an Inverness-shire family. Chisholm already had the lands of Bhlàraidh, Inchbrine, Lochletter and Dulshangie in Glenurquhart and Invermoriston from his grant from the third earl of Moray, and he also inherited his grandfather's lands of Abriachan and Achmony in Glenurquhart, Quarrelwood near Elgin and others.

Sir Robert Chisholm was not just the constable of Urquhart; he also held the positions of sheriff of Inverness, justiciar of the regality of Moray and, like his grandfather before him, justiciar of the north. He was powerful enough to stand up to the Church in a dispute about the rights to milling grain from his Quarrelwood estates. In 1364 his daughter, Janet, married Hugh Rose of Kilravock. Such was the standing of Chisholm that the contract of marriage was executed in the presence of the bishops of Moray and Ross, William, earl of Ross. Sir Robert's son, Alexander, married Margaret, heiress of the Aird, starting the long association of the Chisholms with Strathglass and effecting their transformation into a Highland clan.

While Sir Robert Chisholm was never called on to defend Urquhart from attack, this is not to say that he did not have problems to face during his tenure. While his grandfather had defended the castle in the name of the king, Chisholm's problems came from the king and his family. In 1359, the same year that Chisholm became constable, David II granted the barony of Urquhart to his brother-in-law, William, earl of Sutherland. This seems to have been a highly political act, intended to counter the growing power of the Stewarts. Robert Stewart, the king's nephew, had been recognized as David II's heir presumptive since the 1320s, and the grant of Urquhart to the earl of Sutherland, father of another of David II's nephews, may have been intended to bring about a greater balance of power in the kingdom. The earl of Sutherland's tenure of Urquhart lasted for 11 years, from 1359 to 1370, until, with the death of the earl, the barony again reverted to the Crown. The period covering the earl of Sutherland's ownership seems to have made as little difference to the expansion of Stewart influence as it did to Chisholm's control and management of the barony.

49 *Penny from the reign of King Robert II found at Urquhart*

With the death of David II in 1371, the Crown passed to Robert II, the first of the Stewart kings (**49**). Robert II governed by conciliation rather than command, a practice which was exploited by his large family and other nobles. Urquhart was granted to David, earl of Strathearn, the king's fourth son. Like the earl of Sutherland before him, the earl of Strathearn seems to have made little direct impact on Urquhart. However, in 1384 a flurry of property exchanges suggests a period of considerable upheaval in the area. In that year the earl of Strathearn granted the barony and castle of Urquhart in feu to his elder brother, Alexander, earl of Buchan. In the same year Sir Robert Chisholm surrendered the lands that he held in Glenurquhart and Invermoriston, and they were then also granted to the earl of Buchan. Finally, two years later, Sir Robert surrendered the lands of Achmony and Abriachan, which he held from the bishop of Moray, and these too were granted to the earl of Buchan. The rapacity of the earl of Buchan earned him the sobriquet of the 'Wolf of Badenoch'. As the son of Robert II and the brother of the even less effectual Robert III, Alexander Stewart, earl of Buchan, acted with an impunity that was remarkable even for those turbulent times.

Within a year of making over Urquhart to Alexander, it would appear that the earl of Strathearn was regretting it, complaining to Parliament about Alexander's violent possession of the barony and failure to pay the requisite rents. The earl complained at a distance about his brother's disregard for the law, but the bishop of Moray suffered directly at the earl of Buchan's hands with the burning of Elgin and its cathedral in 1390. Sir Robert Chisholm's abdication of his lands in Glenurquhart should probably be seen as a necessary accommodation of this volatile new owner of the castle and barony. However, Sir Robert seems to have succeeded in creating a workable relationship with the earl of Buchan such that his grandson, Sir Thomas Chisholm, succeeded him as constable of Urquhart. In 1389, Sir Thomas, along with the earl of Sutherland, stood as surety for the earl of Buchan when, in the church of the Dominican Friary in Inverness, he was ordered to send away his mistress and to be reconciled with his wife, Euphemia, countess of Ross.

Life under the constables

50 Surviving pockets in the masonry show the size of the massive joists which supported the floor of the Great Chamber.

The 14th century saw the castle at its peak. It had not yet suffered the ravages of the conflict that surrounded the MacDonald battles for Ross, or the ensuing fall of the lordship of the Isles. Indeed, the 14th century saw the complex at Urquhart undergo continued enhancement, as substantial new masonry buildings were added to the structures built under the Comyns. Unlike many castles further south, Urquhart was subject to comparatively little military action in this period. It did not change hands between rival parties but had a smooth succession between magnates, with continuity emphasized by the succession of constables.

Castles such as Urquhart were not just defensive sites; they were also seats of local government and baronial residences. The Comyn castle, like its contemporaries, Bothwell and Kildrummy, contained a great hall and a separate keep. This arrangement reflected the separation between the public space of the great hall and the private space of the keep. The great hall was the theatre for the public functions of the barony: the courts of justice, the assessment of tributes, the formal feasting of the lord in front of his

51 The courtyard wall of the kitchen. The taller section of the wall to the right is later, with the kitchen originally having a symmetrical façade of a central door flanked by a pair of windows

52 This large structure added to the end of the kitchen could only be entered from outside the watergate. Its purpose is not known

retine. The keep provided the high-status lodgings to which only the lord's family and close circle of associates would have access.

In the 14th century this rigid distinction between the public hall and the private keep becomes blurred. At Urquhart, as at many other castles, it became common for a private chamber to be provided adjacent to the hall. At Urquhart a large structure was added to the north of the great hall, which may have housed this sort of accommodation. This chamber block was constructed with thinner walls than the hall, presumably because it was a less ambitious structure. All that survives is its basement walls, which still show the pockets for the massive timbers used to support the main floor of the building (**50**). With good supplies of local timber, it is not surprising to see such large beams being used to span across a 10m (33ft) space, which, in many similar castles, would have been vaulted. However, it is safe to assume that the first floor was supported by at least one row of timber columns running the length of the space, and that the floors above are likely to have been subdivided to some extent by timbers too.

To the south of the great hall a kitchen was added; its water inlet still survives. The basements of both the hall and the chamber block were accessed by a single door, with the rest of their basements concealed by the rock outcrop. At the kitchen the entire basement was visible, and part of the façade remains. It is a simple, balanced frontage of a central doorway flanked by a pair of windows. Although stone robbing has removed the window surrounds, the dressings of the door and the care taken in the symmetry indicate that, even at the basement level, the construction was intended to satisfy aesthetic sensibilities as well as functional needs (**51**).

An early addition to the kitchen was the enigmatic structure to its south. This addition does not seem to communicate with any other parts of the castle, having its only opening out through the east curtain to the small bay below the watergate. The walls of this extension are buttressed to cope with the lack of a first floor on the inside. The function of the building is unclear, but it would appear to have been related to loch usage; too high above the water to function as a boathouse, it may have been designed for the drying or storage of sails or nets (**52**).

To the south of the watergate a new building was constructed on a tight ledge over the loch. It was suggested in the 1920s that this building had housed a smithy. Very little of this structure survives other than the south gable but this rises to a fragment of wall-walk and incorporates a garderobe chute. The west wall of the building stands less than a metre high and is distinguished by slots for four large upright timbers. Like the great chamber, this building may well have made extensive use of wood, with much of its superstructure being timber-framed rather than stone-built. It is possible that this building was originally intended to provide ancillary accommodation for the shell keep, but it is difficult to pin it to a particular place in the occupation sequence (**53**).

The confident expansion of the buildings at Urquhart during the 14th century is a mark of the success of the Lauder and Chisholm constables. Other than the 1334 siege, there is little recorded military action at Urquhart and it is possible to see the castle largely as a baronial seat and the centre of an extensive estate rather than as a military garrison. However, there are aspects of this history that prevent this assessment from slipping into the cliché of a wealthy castle nobly governing a peaceful land. For a start, the land was not peaceful. Despite the efforts of Thomas Randolph and others, the Wars of Independence were followed by repeated waves of violent lawlessness, which would plague the Highlands for centuries to come. Furthermore, this was a barony where, for much of the time, the baron is likely to have been absent: even when Urquhart was not in the direct possession of the Crown, those who held the barony had their principal estates or residences elsewhere. However, Sir Robert Lauder and his descendants were a family of some substance themselves: both Sir Robert Lauder and Sir Robert Chisholm held the post of justiciar of the north, and for all intents and purposes, Lauder and his successors were the *de facto* barons of Urquhart through the 14th century.

Information from excavations

The clearance excavations of the 1920s and the research excavations on the southern summit in the 1980s produced a large number of finds to shed light on the routine life at Urquhart. They included pottery, animal and fish bones, antler, iron and other metal objects, coins, weapons and personal effects. While few of the objects are as attractive as the bronze ewer or the various brooches found together on the southern summit, they can give us an insight into life at Urquhart.

We know that cattle formed the majority of the inhabitants' livestock, with sheep and goats also making up a significant proportion. Given the cultural importance of cattle as a sign and form of wealth in the medieval Highlands it is not surprising that cattle were generally allowed to live longer before they were slaughtered than the sheep, which rarely lived longer than two years. This is likely to have been fairly characteristic of most of the Highlands at this time. However, some of the finds mark Urquhart out as distinctive. Almost 10 per cent of the bones found at Urquhart were from deer. This is a far higher proportion than is found in the burghs of the time and reflects the importance of hunting within the bounds of the barony. Hunting was not just a source of meat; it was also an activity that was hedged around with cultural meaning. Hunting was a pastime exclusive to the nobility, and thereby became not only a mark of their high status, but almost a duty; a noble who failed to hunt was not meeting social expectations. The barony of Urquhart, covering an enormous area with comparatively little agriculture, was well suited to good hunting and this is likely to have been a distinguishing feature for those holders of the barony who had several estates. Hunting estates were not entirely a 19th-century invention: the Fraser lands of Stratherrick, on the other side of Loch Ness, were prized by their owners for the quality of the hunting, and it is likely that Urquhart offered similar attractions.

The other key food resource that one might expect Urquhart to be making use of was Loch Ness itself. Fish formed an important part of the diet in the Middle Ages, partly because of the requirement to avoid eating meat on a Friday or during Lent.

53 The large slots in the wall of the smithy probably held large beams supporting a timber structure above

Castles and abbeys often had fishponds specifically designed to provide a ready supply of fresh fish throughout the year, but this would not have been necessary with a substantial loch nearby. Our evidence for fish consumption at Urquhart comes from the excavations in the 1980s. However, at the time smaller fish bones were not retrieved by sieving, so our evidence is restricted to the larger species of fish. Of the locally available freshwater fish, salmon and trout appear to have been the most popular. In the 18th century it was noted that the people of Inverness would not eat eels or pike and this practice appears to be reflected in medieval Urquhart. However, the majority of fish being eaten at Urquhart was not caught locally but was cod, caught in the North Sea, salted and shipped inland. The reason for this heavy use of deep-sea fish was the convenience of not needing to rely on catches of fresh fish through the year.

Other finds at Urquhart indicate a more cosmopolitan aspect to life within its walls. Gaming pieces and the tuning pegs of musical instruments remind us of the pastimes of the inhabitants (**54**). Stained-glass fragments indicate the quality of furnishings that adorned the naked buildings. Pottery from the Rhine and the Low Countries would have had a cachet of exclusivity. The consumption of exotic imports would have extended to the foodstuffs and fabrics that trade across the North Sea could bring to Inverness. Inverness was the key supply centre for Urquhart, with goods being brought to the castle by boat and goods from the estate being sold in the

54 Bone gaming piece decorated with a horseman

burgh in turn. We know that timber was a significant market product for the area, but Boece, in his 16th-century *Chronicle of Scotland*, records that the area around Loch Ness also exported furs of beaver, pine marten and fox, among others. The survival of continental pottery at Urquhart, in greater proportions than is found in a trading port such as Inverness, is a good example of the way in which a major castle was an important node in international trade. It acted as a gathering point for the produce of the barony before the excess was shipped on to Inverness for onward sale, and it consumed the speciality goods that overseas traders brought to towns like Inverness.

Excavations at Urquhart in the last ten years have been largely confined to the area outside the walls of the castle. It would be expected that the slopes facing the castle would have been kept clear of structures for defensive reasons. It was therefore surprising to find a sizeable timber building roughly 30m (100ft) east of the south end of the ditch. The building measured roughly 20m by 7m (65ft by 23ft) and pottery found within it seems to date from the 13th to the late 15th century. The north end of the building may have been domestic accommodation, with a timber floor, but the south end is thought to have been a workshop, possibly for a blacksmith. Further analysis is still to be carried out on the finds so any conclusions so far are tentative. Until we have a firmer grasp on the function and the date of the building we cannot understand its relation to what may have been going on within the castle walls.

MacDonald expansion

The rapacious earl of Buchan (aka the 'Wolf of Badenoch') seems to have died in 1394. However, it was the death of his wife that had a greater impact on Glenurquhart. Euphemia was countess of Ross in her own right, and her marriage to the Alexander Stewart appears to have been yet one more act motivated by his insatiable greed for land, wealth and power. When she died, in February 1395, she left two children from her first marriage to Sir Walter Leslie: Alexander, the new earl of Ross, and Mariota, the wife of Donald, lord of the Isles. Alexander was married to Isabella, daughter of Robert III's brother, the duke of Albany, which thereby maintained a strong Stewart interest in Ross.

The late 14th century in the Highlands was a particularly lawless time. There were struggles for supremacy between the emergent clans; figures of authority, such as the earl of Sutherland, were still struggling to bring about an order derived from the Crown; and the earl of Buchan, the most powerful magnate in the North, had deliberately sought to engender fear and havoc for his own profit. In such an atmosphere it is not surprising that the death of the earl of Buchan and the countess of Ross led to unrest. Buchan's illegitimate son, Alexander, the future earl of Mar, continued his father's lawlessness with attacks on both Aberdeen and Forfar, and Alasdair Carrach, brother of Donald, lord of the Isles, staged an attack on Urquhart in 1395.

The MacDonald attack of 1395 fits into a pattern of expansion along the Great Glen that dates back to the start of the 14th century. Under Robert I, the MacDonalds were one of the principal beneficiaries of the redistribution of the MacDougall estates, with Lochaber (along with Morvern and Ardnamurchan) being granted to Angus Óg, father of John, first lord of the Isles. However, in 1322, Thomas Randolph was confirmed in possession of the former Comyn lordship of Lochaber, possibly at the expense of the MacDonalds. The Randolph grant appears to have been enacted, since in 1334 David of Strathbogie, in support of Edward Balliol, is recorded as invading the earl of Moray's Lochaber lands and claiming them as the Comyn heir.

The 14th century witnessed the flowering of the MacDonald lordship of the Isles. 'Good' John, the first MacDonald lord of the Isles, sought consciously to emulate Somerled's kingdom of the Isles, when the western seaboard had been united under a single, largely autonomous ruler. While John's father, Angus Óg, had received a share of the MacDougall territories in return for his support of Robert the Bruce, John saw no need to bind his allegiance to the ruling house. In 1336, the same year that he first used the title *Dominus Insularum*, John was willing to recognize Edward Balliol as king in return for the grant of further lands in the west. Even with the return of David II to Scotland in 1341, such dealings did John's territorial ambitions no harm. In 1343, John made his peace with the king and, in return, was confirmed in possession of the lands that he had received from Edward Balliol.

Three years later saw a further expansion of the lordship's territories, when Ranald MacRuairi, John's brother-in-law, was murdered at Elcho Priory by William, earl of Ross. Only four years earlier, Sir Robert Lauder had hosted at Urquhart the signing of a charter by the earl of Ross in Ranald's favour. John moved swiftly, claiming the MacRuairi lands in the name of his wife, Amy, and thereby consolidating his territories to include Islay, Jura, Colonsay, Mull, Coll, Tiree, Lewis, Uist, Morar, Morvern, Duror, Glencoe and Lochaber. In 1350, John made another shrewd alliance by putting aside his wife Amy in order to marry Margaret Stewart, daughter of the future Robert II. As well as bringing Kintyre into the lordship, this move helped to create a network of political alliances which strengthened the autonomy of the lordship in the face of attempts by the Crown to exert its control. David II's need for taxation to pay for his English ransom brought the Crown and the lordship into direct dispute. John's refusal to allow his lands to be assessed led to an act of revocation affecting Lochaber in 1367 and, eventually, to John's submission to David at Inverness in 1369. While John handed over hostages to the king at Inverness, he succeeded in not losing any territories.

The creation of a single territory under the direction of single magnate on the western seaboard had an impact on the rest of the Highlands. Decades of war had left Scotland highly militarized. Argyll and the Islands had often provided troops to fight elsewhere in Scotland and Ireland and the creation of a unified lordship left them with few opportunities on their home territories. Lochaber, controlling one end of the Great Glen, provided an opening for expansion on mainland Scotland. The failure of the Crown to create a position to wield the same power as the Randolph earls of Moray, following the death of the third earl in 1346, meant that there was no meaningful bulwark to MacDonald expansion along the Great Glen.

The Brae Lochaber, the area that includes Glen Spean and Glen Roy, was given by John to his son Alasdair Carrach, probably in the 1370s, and in effect control over the principal route from Lochaber into Badenoch. John made further land grants to the Clan MacLean, who were granted extensive lands in Morvern and were the most faithful of the lordship's vassal clans. By the closing decades of the 14th century, Lochaber was firmly held as a MacDonald territory.

It has been suggested that Alasdair Carrach's attack on Urquhart in 1395 was a pre-emptive strike to stake the MacDonald claim to Ross. However, his motives are unclear: it is unlikely that this was part of the MacDonald claim to the earldom of Ross, which only became a political issue with the death of Alexander Leslie in 1402. Furthermore, the castle was still, essentially, a royal castle rather than part of the earldom of Ross, with Sir Thomas Chisholm's salary as constable being paid by the Exchequer. Of other motives feud cannot be ruled out, nor can simple opportunism – taking advantage of the death of the earl of Buchan to raid and, if possible, grab territory by force.

Whatever the reasons behind the MacDonald attack, it paid off. By the end of the year, Alasdair Carrach had been made the protector of those lands in Glenurquhart that were under the jurisdiction of the regality of Moray or were owned by the Church. The concession, which appears to have been made because the Crown was powerless at this time to drive the MacDonalds out, was promptly exploited by Alasdair. He installed his nephew Tearlach MacLean as constable of the castle and started to distribute these new lands to MacLean and his other supporters. Over the next three years Alasdair used Urquhart as a base for raiding the comparatively fat lands around Inverness. This resulted in Parliament formally placing the barony in the hands of the king. However, there is no evidence that the legislative might of the assembled estates had the slightest effect in Glenurquhart, and it is safe to assume that Alasdair remained in control of Urquhart – a dangerous cuckoo viewed with caution by his neighbours.

The emergence of the clans

Alasdair Carrach was neither the first, nor the last, Highlander who had a reputation for aggression. Alexander Stewart, earl of Buchan, had used an army of Highland 'caterans' (brigands) in his attack on Elgin in 1390. These '*wyld wykkyd Heland-men*' terrified the inhabitants of the east-coast burghs. However, no party had a monopoly on violence in this period, and one event casts a remarkable light on to both attitudes to violence and the emerging relationship between the Highlanders and Lowlanders: a distinction that was only now starting to be recognized (**55**).

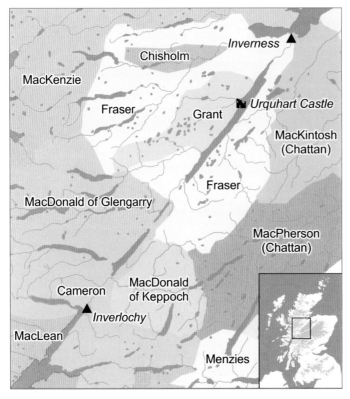

In 1396, on the North Inch at Perth, a gladiatorial combat took place in front of Robert III and the assembled court. The combat appears to have had two functions: entertainment, presumably as an alternative to jousting or bear-baiting, and juridical, as a means of resolving a dispute between two Highland groups. The records for the fight are not clear, but there appears to have been two sides, each of 30 men, although the numbers of one side were made up by buying the fighting services of a local blacksmith, Henry Wynd. The identity of the two groups is open to question, with a variety of clans claiming to have fought at the North Inch. They may have been the Clan Chattan and the Clan Cameron, who were, for many years, in dispute about the lands of Glen Loy and Loch Arkaig. Alternatively, the two sides may have been the MacPhersons and the

Davidsons, both parts of Clan Chattan, who disputed their relative precedence within this confederation. Either way, the fight at the North Inch was a bloody entertainment for the increasingly culturally Lowland court, as all but one of the losing side were killed in front of this audience.

It would appear that from this early period stereotypes of Highlanders were forming, terrifying and thrilling outsiders in equal measure. However, it was a stereotype in which the Clan Chattan, Clan Cameron or whoever was fighting on the North Inch was complicit. The clans that were emerging at the south-west end of the Great Glen (and elsewhere) relied on brutality (and the fear of brutality) to survive, surrounded as they were by likeminded others. Those who had influence over them, such as the earl of Buchan or the lord of the Isles, derived benefit from maintaining militarized lands which recognized the authority of perceived kinship and tradition over the rule of national law.

At the north-east end of the Great Glen clanship developed along a different course. These lands, as far as Abertarff, had been successfully feudalized in the 12th and 13th centuries. They were held by families such as the Chisholms, the Frasers, the Roses and the Grants, who held their land by charter, rather than considering themselves as being an evolution of the family groups who farmed the land. However, both groupings (western clans and eastern families) still had much in common: they were all Highlanders, they shared many cultural values (such as the emphasis on cattle as a form of wealth) and, over the coming centuries, they evolved until the differences between them were no longer readily apparent. What does appear to distinguish these two groupings in this period is their relationship to burghal trade and the allegiances that this brought with it. In simplistic terms, the eastern families held positions in the burghs of the Moray and Cromarty firths and had business interests in these burghs; their interests lay in ensuring peaceful conditions for trade, as could be provided by the Crown. The western clans had no burghs of their own, and viewed the eastern burghs and their hinterlands as rich fruits ready to be plucked by their raiding; they profited from military action, which also suited the expansionist aims of the MacDonald lords of the Isles.

The battle for Ross

Through the 13th and 14th centuries, the major powers in the Highlands were generally the great families who had won their positions of power through service to the Crown – the Durwards, the Comyns, the Randolphs and the Stewarts. The end of the 14th century saw the local powerbrokers of Badenoch, Lochaber and Moray exercise increasing autonomy at the expense of central government. The rapacity of figures such as Alexander Stewart, the earl of Buchan, the ingenious expansionism of the MacDonald cause by men such as Alasdair Carrach and the emergent coherence of the clans such as Chattan and Cameron, had the effect of fragmenting power into smaller, tighter groups, and led to regional insecurity which benefited entrepreneurial lawlessness. Instability leads to change, and by the end of the 15th century the tectonic plates of power in the Highlands had shifted, clashed and reformed; it was a painful century.

In 1402 the death of Alexander Leslie, earl of Ross, allowed Alasdair Carrach to wreak havoc once more. Possibly launching his attack from Urquhart, Carrach's quarry this time was the burgh of Elgin and its cathedral precinct, which he largely destroyed by fire. Leslie had died leaving a young daughter, Euphemia, as his heir, who was promptly taken as a ward by her maternal grandfather, Robert Stewart, duke of Albany and governor of Scotland during the infirmity of Robert III and the captivity of James I in England. It is likely that Alasdair Carrach's attack on Elgin should be seen as a show of force on behalf of his brother, Donald, the second lord of the Isles, in a bid to obtain the wardship of his niece. If so, it was unsuccessful and by October that year, Alasdair and his men returned to Elgin, mouthing contrition and seeking absolution.

However, Albany's control of the young Euphemia clearly continued to unsettle Donald, who may have feared an Albany–Stewart takeover of the earldom of Ross on a par with the irregular acquisition of the earldom of Mar by the earl of Buchan's illegitimate son, Alexander Stewart, in 1404. In 1411 the lord of the Isles' hunger for the earldom of Ross, combined with a possible plot to bring James I back from England, generated a vast army under Donald's command. Much of the army seems to have been raised from the MacDonald lands in the west, and they appear to have met with resistance from the Clan MacKay near Dingwall. This seems to have been little more than a minor annoyance and the army headed south to join with men from the Great Glen clans; they took Inverness before heading towards Aberdeen through Moray. Donald's advance was met at Harlaw, 32km (20 miles) from Aberdeen, by an army of similar proportions commanded on behalf of governor Albany's government by Alexander Stewart, earl of Mar. Battle was joined on 25 July and was famously bloody. The tally of deaths on both sides was so great that it has been said that each side thought the other had won. The result was inconclusive in that there was no clear victor, but it was also decisive in that the effect of such great losses was to stop further warfare. Donald's forces, such as those who survived, retraced their steps, and Mar's forces were in no position to pursue them. The following year Donald submitted to Albany with the only loss appearing to be Alasdair Carrach's tenuous hold on Urquhart – the castle and barony fell into the hands of the earl of Mar.

When Euphemia, countess of Ross, entered a nunnery in 1415, in the eyes of inheritance law she died and her title was taken up by her mother's brother, John Stewart, earl of Buchan. This represented a deviation from the normal course of succession, where the title should have passed to her father's sister, Mariota Leslie, wife of Donald, lord of the Isles. As Donald feared, the Albany Stewarts seem to have managed to usurp the earldom of Ross. However, following Harlaw, Donald seems to have fumed in silence, not making a further move against the powerful governor Albany, the earl of Buchan's father. Perhaps he was biding his time, looking forward to the day when James I could return from England, or to when governor Albany would be succeeded by his less capable son, Murdoch. In 1420, Albany died and Murdoch started to take advantage of his position as governor. On 16th November he signed an indenture with Alexander Stewart, earl of Mar, by which Murdoch offered his protection and assistance to Mar in return for Mar's loyalty and half the income of Glenurquhart.

If Donald was waiting for the return of James I to enable him to make good his claim to Ross, he waited in vain, dying in 1423, the year before James returned from England. Alexander, Donald's son, was proclaimed earl of Ross and lord of the Isles, although this explicit claim to Ross seems to have aroused little attention. In the Highlands, the impact of James's return in 1424 seems to have been felt only gently at first. The king's most pressing priority was to bring order to the kingdom and reduce the power of his cousins, the Albany Stewarts. John Stewart, earl of Buchan, died in France in 1424 and many of the surviving Albany Stewarts were arrested and executed the following year. However, the king's destruction of his cousins did not immediately hand the earldom of Ross over to the MacDonalds, with the title being reserved by the Crown for the rest of James I's reign.

The road to Inverlochy

The impact in the Highlands of James I's personal rule was gradual, with legislation in 1425 and 1426 placing particular duties on the owners of former strongholds in the Highlands to repair them, and through good policing and civilized management of their estates to bring about good order in the north. In 1428, however, James's approach to the Highlands changed gear. In August of that year he summoned a parliament to Inverness. The parliament never sat; its calling was a means by which many of the Highland lords and barons were entrapped. Some were summarily executed as criminals, while Alexander, earl of Ross and lord of the Isles, was taken captive to Perth. Negotiations regarding his future faltered. Alexander escaped, and then vented his anger at the king's betrayal of his subjects' trust by burning the burgh of Inverness and besieging its castle. In carrying out this attack the MacDonalds were assisted by the clans Chattan and Cameron who, like the MacLeans at this period, were clients of the lords of the Isles. James I's parliament of 1424 had passed legislation to formally break such bonds of allegiance between Scotland's families, but such political groupings persisted across the country.

About the same time as the infamous Inverness 'parliament', James appointed a new constable to Urquhart, Thomas Ogilvy of Balfour, who was responsible for both Urquhart and Inverness Castles. The royal accounts record the expenditure of 40 shillings on Urquhart. While this is not a major outlay, it does confirm that from 1428 to 1429 at least, the Crown was taking direct control of this royal castle once more.

The destruction of Inverness was such a flagrant outrage that it had to be dealt with firmly if James's attempt to establish his authority in the north was to be successful. On 23 June 1429, leading an army personally, he met Alexander's army at a place that is only recorded as '*a bog in Lochaber*'. What followed is an interesting example of the conflicting loyalties held by the fighting men of the Highlands and gives us a rare insight into the allegiances of those living in the Great Glen in the 15th century. The presence of the king was sufficient to make the clans Chattan and Cameron desert Alexander in Lochaber; they did not change sides, but they would not raise arms against the person of their anointed ruler. The fact that two entire clans are said to have deserted the lord of the Isles indicates strong clan cohesion. That they were prepared to join the lord of the Isles in sacking a royal burgh and besieging a royal castle indicates that they placed the authority of the MacDonald magnate higher than that of the national government. However, their desertion in the presence of the king's person clearly places the king at the highest point in their loyalties, and shows a preparedness to view the king and national government separately; governments were questionable but loyalty to the king was absolute. Such a distinction between clan, king and government may well foreshadow the later political allegiances of the Lochaber clans.

While the bog in Lochaber was the arena in which the processing of these tensions was played out on a large and dramatic scale, these allegiances and loyalties were part of daily life. A MacLean living in Glenurquhart in the 1420s was bound through ideas of kinship to his clan; this led to an allegiance to the lords of the Isles through his clan's privileged client status. Feudal allegiance, in the form of military service and produce, was due to Alexander Stewart, earl of Mar, the holder of the barony of Urquhart. The interests of national government would be promoted by figures such as Mar but also by office holders such as the sheriff of Inverness and the justiciar of the north. In addition to this, our MacLean clansman would also need to balance the interests of the church and his immediate family. The people of Glenurquhart, in particular, being vulnerable to attack from the west but living in the shadow of a royal castle, must have become adept at negotiating these varying calls on their allegiance.

Within two months of his humiliation in Lochaber, Alexander, lord of the Isles, was at Holyrood Palace, on his knees, making humble submission to the king, following which he was imprisoned in Tantallon Castle. However, this imprisonment brought its own problems in 1431, with Alasdair Carrach, who had received additional territories in Lochaber, being identified, probably correctly, as a continuing source of unrest in the Highlands. Alexander Stewart, earl of Mar, who had for many years been acting as the royal agent in the north, was ordered to bring Carrach to heel and led an army into Lochaber. Carrach had positioned his archers on the slopes to the south of Inverlochy Castle while his cousin, Donald Balloch, brought forces in by sea, trapping Mar's forces and regaining MacDonald honour by a rout of the royal army. It would appear that James simply did not have the resources to reverse this set-back and an accommodation was sought from Alexander, lord of the Isles. This was obtained by the close of the year and the Highlands settled back into its usual turmoil of raiding, counter-raiding and rule by the strongest. It was a political peace, although not a civil one.

The absence of law

The political peace survived until James's death in 1437, at which time Alexander, once again, flexed the muscles of Clan Donald to take advantage of the weakness of the Crown as the six-year-old James II took the throne. And once again it was the lands of the barony of Urquhart that felt MacDonald steel. Thanks to this raid the Clan Donald regained control of Urquhart and Glenmoriston, although the castle did not fall and remained in the hands of the constable, Thomas Ogilvy. Since Alasdair Carrach's tenure of Glenurquhart in the 1390s there had been a branch of the MacLean family in the area descended from Carrach's nephew, Tearlach MacLean. Eachuinn (Hector) Buidhe MacLean, probably Tearlach's son, was now made chamberlain of Urquhart, responsible for the estate but not the castle.

Eachuinn Buidhe's own stronghold was the Castle of Bona or Caisteal Spioradan, at the mouth of Loch Ness, controlling the ford at the start of the River Ness. Caisteal Spioradan, 'the castle of the spirits', earned its name from the ghastly outcome of one of Eachuinn's raids upon his neighbours. Eachuinn was not unique among his contemporaries in earning a good living directing predations on his neighbours. Raiding was an established part of Highland life, and a clan prospered or declined depending on its abilities and those of its leaders to defend their lands, raid and counter-raid. Following the MacDonald loss of Glenurquhart after the Battle of Harlaw, the Urquhart MacLeans had sought alliances with Clan Chattan and Eachuinn had married a granddaughter of the chief of that clan. The long rivalry between the clans Chattan and Cameron is said to have given Eachuinn a reason (not that he is likely to have needed one) to raid Cameron lands deep into Lochaber. The MacLeans returned to their own lands bearing their booty and Cameron hostages. The Camerons gave chase and succeeded in capturing some of the MacLean raiding party, including two of Eachuinn Buidhe's sons. In front of the Castle of Bona, Donald Dubh of Lochiel presented Eachuinn with a choice: exchange hostages or see his sons hang. It is not clear what exchanges took place in the negotiations – both sides blame the other – but the result was that Eachuinn's sons were hanged in front of the walls of his castle, and he retaliated by slaughtering every one of the hostages he held.

Neither the MacLean nor the Cameron versions of this story refer to any recourse to justice, only that the ghosts of the hostages haunted Caisteal Spioradan and led to its abandonment. The story is typical of dozens, if not hundreds of similar stories from the various clan histories that recount the conflicts arising out of raiding. They are characterized by partiality (an excuse is always provided for an apparent act of aggression), bloodshed (great victory, defeat or cataclysm) and a total absence of any reference to the rule of law. While the form of these accounts has been affected by the oral tradition's tendency to eulogize and entertain, they depict a culture where conflict with distant neighbours was commonplace, bringing with it the loss and destruction of life as well as property, and that this was conducted with little interference from the mechanisms of central government that were designed to ensure civil peace.

In the middle of the 1760s, when such raiding had all but ceased, William Lorimer, tutor to the son of the laird of Grant, noted:

> *According to the manners of the old Highlanders, it was not deem'd dishonourable to carry away by force in the night or day time, all the cattle or horses belonging to any person – this was reckoned an Act of Bravery and Courage which was almost their only virtue in esteem among them, arising out of their situation, & the principle of self-preservation which could not be accomplished any other way than by Bravery. But to steal from a person on the highway, was generally reckoned mean & below a Gentleman.*[1]

In short, the Highlands in this period were ruled by clan warlords (gentlemen in their own eyes) who followed their own code of acceptable behaviour, which had little reference to national law. Relying on their military skills and tactical allegiances considerable esteem was to be won by theft and violence within certain socially proscribed bounds.

Urquhart surrounded

Such near-anarchy is perhaps surprising in Glenurquhart given the presence of the castle, normally presumed to be a centre of power and control. As we have seen, from 1411, Glenurquhart and the castle were held by Alexander Stewart, earl of Mar, who was the pre-eminent royal agent in the north in the early 15th century. He was fulfilling the role that the Comyns and the Randolphs had performed in previous centuries, but he did not share their resources and was confronted by far greater problems. At his death in 1435, the castle reverted to the direct control of the Crown (although the estate was soon overrun by the MacDonalds following the king's death two years later). Thomas Ogilvy remained as constable although, for a period at least, the direct management of Urquhart Castle appears to have fallen to Andrew Rede, *customarius* or collector of the Great Custom of Inverness. While the constables of the 13th and 14th centuries appear to have been political and military figures of some substance, Ogilvy and Rede seem to have been administrators, reliable servants of the Crown rather than powerful agents. Managed as an outpost of the royal castle of Inverness, Urquhart seems to have slipped from being a defensive asset to being an administrative issue dealt with by a tax official from the neighbouring burgh.

Between July and September 1447 Rede spent over 40 days at Urquhart during which he authorized the expenditure of £21 12s 4d. This sum included monies for new buildings and repairs to existing ones at both Urquhart and Inverness in preparation for a visit to Inverness of the king. There is no record of the king visiting Urquhart at this time and it is probably safe to assume that the lion's share of expenditure on new building went on works at Inverness Castle. While there is reference to a garrison at Urquhart in 1449, it would appear that Urquhart was a shadow of its former self. Clearly Urquhart was still defensible in 1437, but it is also possible that, powerless to control MacDonald and MacLean activities in the area, it was not worth the effort of capturing.

Urquhart's diminished status in the 15th century was not total; it remained a royal castle and was capable on occasion of accommodating no less a figure than the lord of the Isles himself. However, Urquhart's presence no longer dominated the north-east end of the Great Glen as it had in the 13th century. There was no single reason for this change in fortune but rather a cocktail of social, political and economic factors that were at work on both a local and national scale.

The castle had been adapted through the 14th century to create a closer relationship between the great hall and the private lordly apartments. This reflected a shift in expectations relating to accommodation and social interaction, which was felt across Scotland. However, more radical changes in castle building were still to come, with a growing emphasis on a main tower to which other buildings were increasingly subordinate. The great curtain wall castles such as Urquhart, covering large areas, were built in an age where military action was expected to involve great armies and where great baronial households needed to be accommodated. By the start of the 15th century, conditions in Scotland had changed radically. The weakness of central government across Scotland had led to a fragmentation of power and, while there were still great magnates controlling large swathes of the country, power was increasingly exercised through local agents, lesser nobles or clan leaders. The great households of the Durwards, Comyns or Randolphs had inflated castles like Urquhart to a considerable size. With the dissipation of these large baronial entourages, Urquhart Castle became unwieldy, containing accommodation on an unnecessary scale and with a circuit of walls that, without a large garrison, were defensively flaccid and a liability.

MacDonald invasion

Alexander, earl of Ross and lord of the Isles, died in May 1449 and was succeeded by his 15-year-old son, John. As heir to most of the western seaboard and much of northern Scotland, the marriage of this young man was a keen political issue. His bride was to be Elizabeth Livingston, daughter of Sir James Livingston, the king's chamberlain. Such a match brought benefits to both sides: the earl of Ross gained a creature at the heart of national government and the Livingstons, a family fresh to high office and lacking the stability that comes from large estates, gained a powerful ally. The Livingstons would need this ally since their position at Court was under attack even before the marriage took place. Holding many key court positions but lacking the support of great magnates, the Livingstons fell victim to the young James II's need to establish his authority and replenish the royal coffers. Many members of the family were arrested in September 1449 and by the following March two had been hanged.

The reaction from Clan Donald was renewed insurrection; this time the castles of Urquhart, Inverness and Ruthven in Badenoch fell. As in 1437, the Crown took little action to retrieve these royal possessions, even when Sir James Livingston escaped and was installed as the constable of Urquhart Castle. James II was occupied with power struggles in the south of Scotland with William, earl of Douglas, who, along with the earl of Crawford, had formed a bond of mutual protection with the young earl of Ross's father. Douglas was murdered at the king's own hand; Crawford was defeated in a bloody battle by the earl of Huntly acting in the king's interest. John, earl of Ross and lord of the Isles, seems to have been treated the most leniently of the three, being contained not by force but by emoluments. John was granted Urquhart and its castle in liferent, even though Parliament formally and perpetually annexed the castle and barony of Urquhart to the Crown in 1455.

In 1466 we find John in residence at Urquhart Castle, making a grant of extensive territories in Lochaber to Duncan MacKintosh, chief of Clan Chattan. What is not so clear is what sort of state Urquhart Castle was in. Urquhart had been attacked by the Clan Donald in 1395, 1437 and 1452, and possibly also suffered damage in the earl of Mar's takeover after the Battle of Harlaw in 1411, and in 1429 when MacDonald troops sacked Inverness and caused havoc in the surrounding area. The references to new building and repairs to buildings at Urquhart in 1448 are vague and any renovations could have been very slight. Close examination of the remains at Urquhart does suggest that the great castle built up in the 14th century had received quite some damage over the years. The great hall and its adjacent chamber block and kitchen appear to have suffered the worst. The chamber block was abandoned completely and the great hall seems to have undergone major reconstruction, possibly being adapted to barracks or living accommodation. A garderobe chute now emptied from the upper storeys of the converted hall block into what had been the basement of the great chamber (**56**). As the garderobe could have emptied on to the rocks above the loch, this is an unusual arrangement, suggesting that the ordure was being collected, probably for fertilizer.

56 The base of a garderobe chute constructed in the 15th century in what had been the basement of the Great Chamber

A similar garderobe, emptying within the castle, is found in the massive walls that were inserted into the shell keep at this time. Durward's shell keep was originally filled with timber buildings but its function as the core of the complex was taken over by the Comyn tower and hall in the northern half of the site. The reoccupation of the shell keep at this time may be related to the turmoil of the time. Judging by the thickness of the new walls, the buildings constructed within the shell keep were several storeys high and would have provided the occupants with a position that was more readily defensible without a large baronial host. A large number of finds, many of which are dateable to the 15th century, such as the bronze ewer, have come from the area of the shell keep (**57**). A large number

57 Bronze ewer, or water jug, dating from the 15th century found on the slopes of the southern summit of Urquhart

of small iron artefacts suggests that this material had been gathered together for some reason but the reporting of finds in the 1920s excavations was sporadic, ignoring bone and most pottery, so we have very little context for these finds. However, the amount of material on the southern summit not only indicates occupation during this period, but also raises the possibility that the new buildings within the shell keep suffered destruction so suddenly that the contents could not be removed first.

Urquhart defeated

The information we have from the excavations and the building analysis is fairly vague and must be treated with caution. However, we do know that by 1479, three years after the earldom of Ross was forfeited and the estate and castle returned to direct Crown control (see below), Urquhart and Glenmoriston are recorded as being wholly waste. This suggests that the custody of the estate by the earl of Ross had not been particularly glorious and would accord with a castle that was dilapidated.

The MacDonald forfeiture of the earldom of Ross in 1476 can be seen as the start of a process of bringing into line an over-mighty magnate. While the lords of the Isles had recognized the overlordship of the Stewart kings when necessary, they had a long history of rebellion and plotting with the king's enemies. The final straw was the Treaty of Westminster-Ardtornish. This grandly titled secret pact between John, earl of Ross and lord of the Isles and Edward IV of England had been signed in 1462, but this act of treason did not come to light until 1475. The loss of the earldom of Ross, and other territories including Urquhart and Glenmoriston, was accompanied by a regranting of the title and lands of the lordship of the Isles which made it explicit that the title brought with it no greater autonomy than had any other member of the nobility. While John, lord of the Isles accepted this, his illegitimate son, Angus Óg, along with many other MacDonalds, bridled at this demotion of Clan Donald dignity. The result was civil war in the lands of Clan Donald, with Angus Óg turning his father out of Finlaggan, the seat of the lords of the Isles on Islay, and, eventually, defeating him at the Battle of Bloody Bay near Tobermory in 1481. It may have been the unrest that Angus Óg and his allies brought about that resulted in the lands of Urquhart and Glenmoriston being considered to be entirely waste in 1479.

There were also other, more local tensions in Glenurquhart. Following the forfeiture of 1479, Urquhart and Glenmoriston were placed in the care of the earl of Huntly, who oversaw them as a royal agent. It is worth noting that the Exchequer Rolls, which record the payment of rent for the estate at this time, make no mention of the castle, implying that it was little regarded in comparison with the extensive estates. Huntly promptly let the estates to Hugh Rose of Kilravock but, unsurprisingly in such troubled times, this ran into resistance. Members of the Clan Chattan tried to stake a claim to the estates on behalf of their kinsman Ewen MacLean, son of Eachuinn Buidhe MacLean.

It may be the actions of the Clan Chattan that left the estates so devastated, but by 1481 the position was such that the earl of Huntly called for arbitration. A committee was appointed, comprising Alexander Gordon (son of Huntly), Sir Duncan Grant of Freuchie, his son John, Sir James Ogilvy of Deskford, Alexander MacKintosh of Rothiemurchus and David Ogilvy of Thomade. As most of these men came from families that had built their wealth on the use of charters and respect for national government, it is unsurprising that the MacLean claim to Urquhart and Glenmoriston was rejected by them. This did not prevent Ewen MacLean from continuing to press his claim with force, even attacking the castle of Kilravock. The possession of Urquhart seems to have been too much trouble for Hugh Rose, who exchanged his lease of Urquhart and Glenmoriston for the keepership of Redcastle.

As with the liferent granted to the lord of the Isles in 1451, the sum payable to the Crown was only £100 a year. This was not a huge sum for such a large estate, and the fact that the Urquhart and Glenmoriston could not generate such an amount is a stark display of the dire situation that the farms of the area must have been in. Huntly soon managed to find a new tenant for the estate: Duncan Grant of Freuchie, one of the adjudicators in the dispute regarding the MacLean claim to the area. The Grant of Freuchie estates were mainly on Speyside, around what is now Grantown-on-Spey. The Grants, like the Roses and the Frasers, were one of the eastern families who had established themselves in the Highlands with feudal charters and who, generally, had respected Crown authority. The Grants had first had lands in the area of Loch Ness in the 14th century, owning the lands of Stratherrick before they became part of the Fraser estates.

John Grant, known as *am Bard Ruadh* (the Red Bard), inherited the Grant estates from his grandfather Duncan in 1485, although he may well have been trying to manage Urquhart and Glenmoriston from 1482. As with the Roses of Kilravock, he appears to have run into opposition from the MacLeans: local tales told of the MacLeans killing one of the Grant men and washing his head in mac Uian's pool beneath the Bridge in Drumnadrochit before sending it as an intimidating gift to the laird of Freuchie. Grant's difficulties in running the estate are reflected in the rents that he paid to the earl of Huntly; they were halved until 1496 because the MacDonalds in Glenmoriston deliberately disrupted the running of the estate and, judging by a dispute with his landlord in 1492, even the reduced sum was not often forthcoming from John Grant.

While the Red Bard may not have been a perfect tenant, he did make headway in bringing about a closer regard for the rule of law on the estates. In 1498, James IV expressed his gratitude to John for bringing to justice Allan Mór mac Ewen (probably the son of Ewen MacLean). Four years later John's landlord changed, with his lease now being held directly from the Crown rather than going through the earl of Huntly. This new lease allowed Grant to keep £20 out of the £100 a year rent to offset his costs in the upkeep of the castle. It would appear that before this date Grant's lease had simply covered the farms of the barony. Over the previous 20 years, Grant seems to have succeeded in demonstrating his reliability and receiving the care of a royal castle, albeit a neglected one, should be seen as a mark of that achievement.

The Red Bard's success merits some explanation. Since the 1390s the Crown had spectacularly failed to exert any real authority in the barony of Urquhart; either the estates had been controlled by the Clan Donald or their allies the MacLeans, or the estates had been held with some discomfort by great magnates such as Alexander Stewart, earl of Mar or the third earl of Huntly. In one way, Grant was the beneficiary of good timing; political (as opposed to civil) unrest in the Highlands and Islands was gradually reduced in this period. Helped by the assassination of Angus Óg, the rebellious son of John, lord of the Isles, in Inverness in 1490, James IV and his lieutenants general, the earls of Huntly and Argyll, went on to break the effective power of Clan Donald, fragmenting its leadership between rival families. However, Grant also occupied much the same position in local society as that held by the successful 14th-century constables, Sir Robert Lauder and Sir Robert Chisholm. While Grant may not have been from Urquhart, he was accustomed to Highland sensitivities from his own estates on Speyside, and he did not have such great national responsibilities that he could not devote time and effort to the management of the barony. By 1502, he was trading in the furs of pine martens directly with the royal household, which suggests a close level of involvement in the running of the estate. Although Castle Grant on Speyside remained his main residence, Balmacaan in Glenurquhart seems to have become the centre of estate business about this time.

---

[1] Notes made by William Lorimer, tenant of Moulinearn near Dunkeld, and tutor to Sir James Grant, in 4 notebooks, National Archives of Scotland. GD248/37/4/3. The underlining is Lorimer's.

6

The tower – a residence for the Grants

58 Places referred to in the 1509 grants of the baronies of Urquhart, Corrimony and Glenmoriston. The distribution suggests that the lands of the royal barony of Urquhart were the same as the parish. 1 Achlain; 2 Achtemarack; 3 Balmacaan; 4 Bhlàraidh; 5 Borlum; 6 Bunloit; 7 Clunemor; 8 Clunemor; 9 'Conechane'; 10 Corrimony; 11 Craskie; 12 Culnakirk; 13 Dalchriechart; 14 Delshangie; 15 Divach; 16 Drumbuie; 17 Dundreggan; 18 Gartaly; 19 Inchbrine; 20 Invermoriston; 21 Inverwick; 22 Kerrowgair; 23 Lochletter; 24 'Mekle-Deveauch'; 25 Pitkerrald Croy; 26 Polmaily; 27 St Ninian's; 28 The Four 'Mekleis'

On 8 December 1509, at Stirling Castle, James IV removed an old thorn from the side of the Scottish kings: he gave away Urquhart. Since the late 14th century Urquhart had been a problem for the Crown: a royal possession where royal authority had little effect. The period of John Grant's lease of the estates had seen real progress in advancing the civil peace necessary for the area to prosper. In modern terms, and indeed in the view of much of the Lowlands at the time, life in the Great Glen remained dangerous and violent, but for the first time in over a hundred years the greater strength now resided with those who used the law rather than force alone to advance their position. The Grant tenure of Urquhart appeared to have made a difference and in order to consolidate this position, reward the Red Bard and offload this troublesome property lest conditions deteriorate, James had the estates split into three baronies for John and two of his sons.

The 1509 grant of lands to Freuchie and his sons

John Grant, the Red Bard, received the barony of Urquhart, which included the castle and the lands of Borlum, St Ninians, Kerrowgair, Drumbuie, Balmacaan, Gartaly, Polmaily, Delshangie, Inchbrine, 'Mekle-Deveauch' (probably at Divach in Glencoiltie)

58 Places referred to in the 1509 grants of the baronies of Urquhart, Corrimony and Glenmoriston. The distribution suggests that the lands of the royal barony of Urquhart were the same as the parish. 1 Achlain; 2 Achtemarack; 3 Balmacaan; 4 Bhlàraidh; 5 Borlum; 6 Bunloit; 7 Clunemor; 8 Clunemor; 9 'Conechane'; 10 Corrimony; 11 Craskie; 12 Culnakirk; 13 Dalchriechart; 14 Delshangie; 15 Divach; 16 Drumbuie; 17 Dundreggan; 18 Gartaly; 19 Inchbrine; 20 Invermoriston; 21 Inverwick; 22 Kerrowgair; 23 Lochletter; 24 'Mekle-Deveauch'; 25 Pitkerrald Croy; 26 Polmaily; 27 St Ninian's; 28 The Four 'Mekleis'

and Bunloit south of Urquhart Castle (58). The new barony of Urquhart effectively encompassed Glenurquhart, from Loch Meiklie to Loch Ness. John's eldest, but illegitimate, son, John Mor, received the new barony of Glenmoriston, which included the lands of 'Conechane' (probably Achnaconeran), Craskie, 'Euachcur', Achlain, Dalchreichart, Dundreggan, Inverwick, Bhlàraidh and Invermoriston. However, it also included the lands of Culnakirk and half of Clunemor in Glenurquhart. The barony of Corrimony was given to John Og, the second legitimate son of the Red Bard (his eldest legitimate son received nothing but was his father's heir). His lands included Corrimony itself, 'Morull', the four 'Mekleis' (lands around the west end of Loch Meiklie including Shewglie), Lochletter, Achtemarack, and, as with John Mor's possessions, some properties in the eastern end of Glenurquhart: Pitkerrald Croy, Divach and half of Clunemor.

The breaking up of the estates of Urquhart into three baronies could have been an attempt to lessen the chances of a single man wielding too much power in the area. However, it is also possible that the intention was that by having smaller estates it was more likely that the trusted owner would live in the vicinity of his tenants, thereby enhancing the laird's ability to have a beneficial effect on his barony. The terms of the charters make it clear that these new baronies were being created

> *for the benefit of the state and progress and to have good order among the inhabitants and for making those obedient to our laws who in times past have been unruly and unlawful.*[1]

60 *The tower house was built reusing the base of the earlier Comyn tower*

As well as paying a feu duty to the king for the baronies, and providing military service in the form of three horsemen for every £10 of land, there were other stipulations, which were related to the rehabilitation of the estates. The Red Bard was required to:

> repair or build at the Castle a tower, with an outwork or rampart of stone and lime, for protecting the lands and the people from the inroads of thieves and malefactors; to construct within the castle a hall, chamber, and kitchen, with all other requisite offices, such as a pantry, bakehouse, brewhouse, barn, oxhouse, kiln, cot, dove-grove and orchard, with the necessary wooden fences; to reclaim and labour untilled land lying in meadows or under pasture; to make 'stiling' or enclosures; to improve the King's highway within the Barony; to cultivate hemp and flax; to watch over such matters of common advantage as stone and wooden bridges, 'faldyettis' [cattle folds], and stiles; to provide common passage through the lands and Barony.[2]

59 *The inner close was formed by the construction of two new buildings next to the tower. The courtyard level was levelled, burying the tower's basement*

The Grant buildings

This list of requirements is unlikely to have come as a surprise to John Grant who, presumably, was involved in the detail of drafting the charters. The building works at the castle are what would be expected for a country residence of a man of substance at the start of the 16th century. They are also an indication of the poor condition of the castle by this time. Given the requirement for outworks of stone and lime, it would appear that the curtain wall was no longer tenable; it was probably breached in places. As such it would appear that the castle was no longer able to act as a defence '*from the inroads of thieves and malefactors*'. Under John Grant, Urquhart was transformed from a largely defunct medieval castle to a defensible tower-house residence, better suited to the needs of the new laird (**60**).

The starting point for Grant's new residence was the 13th-century tower at the north end of the site. This was adapted to provide a small hall above the existing cellar, with a further chamber on each of the two floors above. Around the tower was created a small cobbled courtyard. To create a fairly level surface for this inner close, the ground was raised to bury the basement of the tower, whose first floor entrance could now be reached directly. (The ditch now visible in front of the tower was created by the excavations of the Ministry of Works in 1921 to reveal the basement's window.)

Along the south and west sides of the inner close two new buildings were constructed (**59**). The building to the west had a fireplace at each end, indicating that it was subdivided into two. Simpson had identified the building as housing a kitchen, and its location, close to the tower but separate from it in case of fire breaking out, would suit this purpose. However, neither of the two fireplaces are of the size that one would expect for a kitchen of this date. The building to the south of the tower was built reusing the footings of the earlier latrine tower and the 14th-century great chamber. The only feature that has survived in this building is a small window in its west gable. Between this building and the tower is a fragment of walling, which would appear to contain the base of a bread oven. Kitchens and bakehouses were often built near each other and it is quite possible that these new buildings on the south side of the inner close were the location for cooking, baking and brewing.

This inner close and tower house occupied only a small proportion of the area of the medieval castle. A wall was built across the narrow waist of the site to cut off the southern half, which appears to have been largely abandoned. Indeed, the lack of activity in this area had benefits, being conducive to the raising of pigeons in a newly constructed 'beehive' dovecot (**61**). The gatehouse appears to have remained in use, providing additional accommodation (possibly the cots mentioned in the charter) and a first line of defence against raiders.

The Great Glen in the 16th century

The Grants, as owners of the new baronies of Urquhart, Corrimony and Glenmoriston, were comparative newcomers to the Great Glen, and the refurbished castle at Urquhart was a very visible signal of this new presence. John Og and John Mor made their more modest homes at Corrimony and Tom an t-Sabhail, near Dundreggan in Glenmoriston, respectively but each of the major families in the Great Glen had a principal seat of some description.

Inverness remained a royal castle and James IV spent considerable sums on its upkeep and improvement, probably adding the great tower house that dominated the burgh until the late 18th century (**62**). At the other end of the Great Glen, Inverlochy was placed in the charge of the earl of Huntly. While the large structures of Inverness and Inverlochy, as royal castles, served as barracks for garrisons and courthouses, the leaders of the various clans in the glen required homes that were secure from attack. On the remains of the motte of Thomas of Thirlestane at Abertarff, the Frasers may have built a small tower, probably for intermittent use rather than as a residence. The MacDonalds of Keppoch seem to have done much the same thing in constructing the Old House of Keppoch on the top of their earlier motte.

61 Beehive dovecot at Aberdour Castle, Fife. The 16th-century dovecot at Urquhart was of a similar design

Torcastle in the Lochaber seems to have started life as a stronghold of one of the families that made up the Clan Chattan, possibly the seat of the MacKintosh chief (**63**). However, it lay within the lands that the Camerons occupied and which led to their enduring feud with the Clan Chattan. It appears that the Camerons built a small tower on this naturally defensible rock but did not rely on it alone for their security. At the mouth of Loch Eil sits the island of Eilean nan Croabh, known in the 16th century as the Isle of Loch Eil, on which stood the residence of the clan chief. The Camerons also had an island site on Loch Arkaig. Eilean Loch Aircaig is thought to be largely man-made, possibly being a substantial earlier crannog on which the Camerons constructed a chapel dedicated to St Columba. The need for a chapel on a defensible site may stem from the attack of Clan Chattan on Palm Sunday 1423 or 1424, when the church in which the Camerons were worshipping was burnt down, almost wiping out the leaders of the clan. The

62 Inverness in the late 17th Century. John Slezer's view shows the royal castle on the hill to the right and the remains of Cromwell's citadel to the left

90

Camerons were not alone in the Great Glen in using island sites; the Castle of Bona, Caisteal Spioradan, may have started life as an island, and their defensive qualities are obvious, especially in inland waters where large boats are rare.

The MacDonalds of Glengarry appear to have made particular use of this practice. Timothy Pont's manuscript maps of various parts of Scotland, prepared in the late 16th century, show Loch Oich in some detail (**63**). The map makes no mention of Invergarry Castle but shows two crannogs in Loch Oich with buildings on Eilean Drynachan and 'ylen Innergarry', now known as Eilean na H-Ealaidh. This island sits just below the Raven Rock on which Invergarry Castle was built in the 17th century, and appears to have been the former seat of the clan. The MacDonald use of crannogs should not be seen as anachronistic but rather as a common response to the need for security in the Highlands at the time. Indeed, there are few crannogs in the Great Glen that do not appear to have been occupied in some way in the 16th century, with Pont showing a building on Eilean Muireach or Cherry Island, the only crannog in Loch Ness.

Little is known about the history of these late crannogs, but some have stories attached that go some way to explaining the variety of uses to which they were put. On Loch Lundie, in the hills to the north of Invergarry, Pont's map shows an occupied crannog – Eilean Mhic Rhaonuill. This is said to have been the safe house

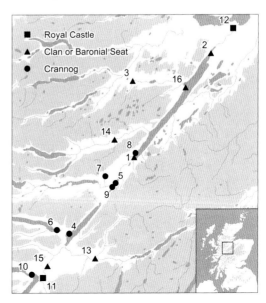

for a notorious MacDonald marauder, Allan of the Red Shirt, who thrived at the start of the 17th century. Not all crannogs should be seen as defensive retreats though; in 1580 the Clan Chattan constructed a crannog in Loch Lochy in the bay of Clunes to use as a base in an aggressive campaign to seize the lands occupied by the Camerons. It was constructed of timbers driven into the loch bed, earning it the name Eilean Darach (Island of the Oaks), although it was also known as Eilean an Toisich. The construction of the Caledonian Canal at the start of the 19th century altered the levels of all the lochs in the Great Glen, and several crannogs no longer rise above the waters.

Politics in the Glen

The death of Angus Og in 1490 and the capture of Donald Dubh in 1503, the only descendant of John, the last lord of the Isles, did not bring to an end hopes for a MacDonald resurgence. Succession among the clans of the West Highlands, such as the MacDonalds, had a strong tradition of tanistry, whereby the successor to a chief could be selected from his relatives on the basis of merit. Several leading men of the clan successively put themselves forward in rebellion to regain the dignity of the lordship. This led to risings under men such as Alexander of Lochalsh in the 1490s and his son Donald Gallda in the 1510s, but also to a general antagonism against the Crown in the West Highlands. The hopes of the MacDonald cause survived until 1543 when Donald Dubh, newly freed from 40 years of captivity, staged a rising in the Western Isles. Supported by Henry VIII of England, the rising was split by internal arguments and dissolved with Donald Dubh's death in 1545.

During the 15th century the Clan Donald had expanded up the Great Glen and consolidated its holding in Lochaber. The MacDonalds of Keppoch and the MacDonalds of Glengarry had established themselves in their respective lands in the Brae Lochaber and to the west and north of Loch Oich, even though the legal documents were slow to recognize this. As with other clans, the members of the Clan Donald were not restricted to the estates of the Clan Donald gentry and a significant population of MacDonalds was also to be found in Glenmoriston.

The Camerons, although firmly established in the lands around the north of Lochiel, around Loch Arkaig and in Glen Loy, were in enduring feud with the Clan Chattan over the same lands. It was a feud that lasted for over three centuries and which the lords of the Isles exploited by using the Clan Chattan to persecute the Camerons. By siding with the Clan Chattan, the lords of the Isles helped ensure they had the support of a clan whose undisputed territories in Badenoch made them a bulwark against the advances of the influence of the national government and the king's lieutenants, the earls of Huntly in particular. The Clan Chattan differed from the other clans in being a confederation of kinship, principally, the MacKintoshes, the MacPhersons and the Davidsons. Originally holding lands in Lochaber, the clan was widely distributed across Badenoch but retained a claim in law to the lands held by the Camerons and the MacDonalds of Keppoch. The clans Donald, Cameron, Chattan and others such as MacLean, while they had their internal differences, were generally united in their opposition to the distant rule of Scotland's kings, casting their lot in with the fortunes of the lords of the Isles or those who subsequently claimed the title. However, at varying times these clans and their subdivisions were fighting to restore the lordship, competing for the chance to contest the lordship, or were busy trying to salvage for themselves as much as possible from the wreck of the lordship. Such divisions led to the West Highlands being a particular source of unrest in the 16th century and gave the Crown both the justification and the opportunity to force its will on the lands formerly dominated by the MacDonald chiefs.

Government power was exercised through agents. Archibald Cameron, second earl of Argyll was given the task of bringing the MacDonald heartlands of Argyll to heel, while in 1501 Alexander Gordon, third earl of Huntly received a similar commission as a royal agent for the north-west. He was particularly charged with enforcing the payment of royal rents in Lochaber, where he was to be consulted on the repairs to the royal castle of Inverlochy. In addition to this, he was in command of various expeditions to the west that crushed Donald Dubh's first rising in 1507.

The rise of the earls of Huntly and the earls of Argyll in the late 15th century had been largely as a result of their service to the Crown in the dismantling of Clan Donald control in the north and west. The first earl of Huntly had received the lordship of Badenoch as early as 1451, and the Gordons, a family originally from the Borders, quickly became the unacceptable face of Lowland expansionism. The Great Glen became a crucial arena for a clash between the cultures of a Gaelic-speaking Highlands, whose principal social divisions were based on perceived kinship, and an English/Scots-speaking Lowlands, where social divisions were based on legal documents. The western clans were threatened from the south by the earls of Argyll while in the Glen Mór itself they were blocked by the Gordon earls of Huntly, the Frasers and the Grants: the Great Glen was once more broken in two halves.

The Great Raids on Urquhart

The premature death of Scotland's kings was an unfortunate habit that the country found hard to break. When James I was murdered in 1437, Alexander, lord of the Isles invaded Urquhart, taking advantage of the uncertainty caused by the succession of a minor. In 1513, James IV died at the Battle of Flodden, leaving an infant as his heir. In a remarkable echo of the events of 1437, Sir Donald Gallda MacDonald of Lochalsh invaded Urquhart, Glenmoriston and Corrimony on the Feast of All Hallows, and held them for three years. John Grant did not seek justice for this at the point of a sword but at the point of a quill, and his appeal to the Lords of Council for recompense survives. Donald Gallda and his accomplices, including the MacDonalds of Glengarry, were accused of taking:

> *pottis, pannis, kettilis, nop* (napkins), *beddis, schetis, blancatis, coueringis, coddis* (pillows), *fische, flesche, breid, aill, cheis, butter, and vyther stuf of houshald, and salt hydis, extending be gude estimatioun to the soume of ane hundreth pund with the mair.*

More importantly, they took 740 bolls of bere (barley) and 1040 bolls of oats (1 boll = approximately 210 litres), 300 cattle and a thousand sheep. Unsurprisingly Donald Gallda and his fellow defendants did not attend the hearings in Edinburgh. In their absence they were ordered to pay £2,000 to John Grant, not just for the loss of goods and livestock but also for the loss of three years' production of the estates.

The list of goods taken suggests a bucolic scene of country life with the MacDonald raiders making off with domestic items and the produce of the land. The raid took place only four years after John Grant received the barony of Urquhart and it is not clear how advanced works were on transforming the castle into the new lairdly seat. The 1513 raid may have been the impetus for the final major change that John Grant made to Urquhart. The focus of the new castle was the tower with its adjacent ranges built around a tight courtyard, supplemented by the great 13th-century gatehouse. This left the remains, probably derelict if not entirely ruinous, of the crescent of buildings formed around the former great hall and the buildings on top of the shell keep. These crumbling buildings would have been considered unsightly and possibly dangerous, providing any raiders with good cover for attacking the tower. They seem therefore to have been systematically demolished; their walls pushed in to fill their basements. It may have been at this point that the building identified as a chapel on the lower, northern summit of the site was cleared. Photographs taken before the 1920s seem to show this summit left with a deliberately flattened top, and it is possible that this summit and the in-filled buildings looking out over the loch were now prepared as platforms for positioning artillery (see illustration **4**). Urquhart Castle would not be so easily overpowered again.

John Grant's recourse to law following the 1513 raid may be seen as the mark of a man who saw the limits of violence as a means to an end. It is possible that one of the qualities that allowed him to make a success of the management of the Urquhart estates in the face of considerable opposition was a certain flexibility, and an awareness of the need to adapt to his new neighbours. In 1510 both the Red Bard and John Mor Grant of Glenmoriston were accused of aiding the king's enemies, possibly as a result of not prosecuting fugitives from justice who had entered their estates. However, in 1520, the Red Bard made a much clearer move to form closer bonds with the other clans in the Glen. In that year his daughter, Agnes, was married to Donald Cameron, the heir to the captaincy of Clan Cameron, and with this wedding came a mutual bond of support and non-aggression between the two families. The Camerons had not been involved in the raid of 1513 and would be a useful ally, with the MacDonald lands of Glengarry now caught between those of Grant and Cameron.

This marriage, while notable, was merely part of the social changes that were transforming the leading figures of families such as the Grants and Frasers into clan chiefs into the mould of the western clans. Many of the tenants of these eastern families were MacDonalds, MacLeans, Camerons or MacKintoshes; they gave their allegiance to the chief of their clan before their landlord. By gradually taking on the trappings of clanship and encouraging their tenants to take the name of Grant, the successive lairds of Freuchie and Urquhart earned the loyalty of people who, in 1509, were merely tenants.

The process, like any social change, was a gradual one and it was perhaps not until the 18th century that the various Highland clans became so similar in their structures that to the outsider the only things that differentiated them was their political allegiance.

The bond of friendship with the Clan Cameron in 1520 did not ensure perpetual peace. John Grant, the Red Bard, died in 1528 and was succeeded by his son, James. James was to be known as Seamus nan Creach, James of the Raids, for reasons that will become apparent. It was James who, in 1544, assisted the earl of Huntly and the Frasers in a large attack on the Clanranald in Moidart. The attack stemmed from a disputed succession; since c.1530 the *de facto* captain of Clanranald had been Iain Mùideartach (John of Moidart), an illegitimate son of one of the leading figures of the family who had been accepted as captain largely because of his personal qualities as a leader. In terms of succession through the legitimate male line, the rightful captain was Ranald Gallda. Gallda translates into English as stranger; Ranald had been brought up not in Moidart, among the Clanranalds, but with the Frasers, his mother's family. In 1540, following the unsuccessful rising of Donald Gorm MacDonald of Sleat, James V had travelled through the West Highlands and, with his ship anchored in Portree harbour, had invited many of the clan chiefs to pay homage. Iain Mùideartach, who had supported Donald, answered the royal summons and walked into a trap. He was taken prisoner by the king, along with Alasdair Mac Iain Mhic Alasdair MacDonald of Glengarry. The absence of the captain of Clanranald gave Hugh Fraser, Lord Lovat the opportunity to put forward his nephew Ranald Gallda as a replacement. Ranald appears to have been accepted due to his birth by the leaderless and uncertain clan.

In 1543 Iain Mùideartach gained his freedom and was welcomed back with open arms by the Clanranald, who drove out Ranald Gallda. There followed a raid by the Clanranald, the Camerons and the MacDonalds of Keppoch on the Fraser lands of Abertarff and Stratherrick, and the Grant lands of Urquhart and Glenmoriston. The response to a raid of this scale was the formation of an army led by the earl of Huntly, comprising 1,500 MacKintosh men from his Badenoch estates in addition to 400 Fraser and Grant men. The Grant presence in this army was not simply a matter of revenge for the 1543 raid but reflected the family bonds between the Frasers and the Grants. Anne Grant, the sister of James, third laird of Freuchie was married to Hugh Fraser, Lord Lovat, whose sister, Isobel Fraser, the mother of Ranald Gallda, took John Mor Grant of Glenmoriston as her second husband. The campaign against the Clanranald seems to have been inconclusive. The raiders who had supported Iain Mùideartach retreated down the Great Glen and, effectively, melted into the mountains of Lochaber. Having reached Inverlochy in pursuit, Huntly's army proceeded no further; Huntly took his troops back to Badenoch through Glen Spean and the Braes of Lochaber while the Frasers and Grants returned along the Great Glen. However, they were intercepted at the head of Loch Lochy by the re-formed Clanranald, Cameron and Glengarry forces.

The Battle of Blar-na-Leine was disastrous for the Frasers and established Iain Mùideartach as the undisputed captain of Clanranald. Hugh Fraser, his young heir, several brothers, Ranald Gallda and, by some accounts, all but five of the Fraser men were cut down in a battle which raged through the heat of the July day. The loss of life on the Fraser part seems to have sated Iain Mùideartach's need for revenge on the Frasers, however the Grants were still to pay for their support.

In October 1544, the lower farms of Invermoriston suffered a raid in which, in its avoidance of the MacDonald tenants in upper Glenmoriston, appears to have been deliberately focused on punishing John Mor Grant for his involvement earlier in the year. However, this raid was simply a minor foretaste of what was to follow. In April 1545, the MacDonald clans of Clanranald, Glengarry, Keppoch and MacIain of Ardnamurchan, assisted by the Camerons, poured into Glenurquhart. They spent the following weeks executing a careful plan of theft and destruction, sparing the lands of Corrimony because the laird had not sent any men to join Huntly and the Frasers the previous year. By the end of May they had burnt down the farmsteads of the glen and '*swept the land of every hoof and article of food or furniture which they could find*'. The surviving tally of goods stolen from the people of Glenurquhart makes this the best documented of any of the Highland raids, as well as, possibly, the most devastating. We have the names of 113 householders distributed across 17 properties and in each case we know what that farmstead lost. For example, Donald McGillendreis, who farmed part of the lands of Drumbuie, lost 10 great cattle, 5 calves, 3 young cattle, 3 horses, 10 yearling sheep, 6 lambs, 12 goats, 8 kids, 40 bolls of oats, 6 bolls of bere (barley) and 14 shillings of furniture. The total for the estates of Glenurquhart was quite staggering:

1,288	*great cattle*
625	*calves*
432	*young cattle*
10	*yearling cattle*
371	*horses*
24	*mares*
1,737	*ewes*
231	*wedders* (castrated rams)
210	*gimmers* (young ewes) *and dinmonts* (young castrated rams)
1,199	*lambs*
1,410	*goats*
794	*kids*
122	*swine*
3,206	*bolls of oats*
1,427	*bolls of bere*
£323 12s 4d	*of furniture*
64	*geese*
60	*ells of cloth*★
£12	*of cash*
2	*plough oxen*

(★ One ell measures a little under one metre.)

In addition to this, the castle itself suffered the loss of:

> *tuelf feddir beddis, with the bowstairs* (bolsters), *blancattis and schetis, price xl^{li}; five pottis, price of thame ten merkis; sax pannys, price ten merkis; ane bascyn, price xiiij s.; any kyst* (chest), *and within the samin three hundreitht pundis of money; two brew calderovnis, price fivetene pundis; sax speittis, price thre pundis; barrellis, standis of attis, pewder weschell, and vuther insycht, to the valour of fourty pundis; twenty pece of artailzery, and ten stand of harnes, price of thame and hundreitht markis; lokkis, durris, zettis* (yetts, iron gates), *stancheovnis, bandis, burdis* (tables), *beddis, chearis, formes* (benches), *and vuther insycht, extending to the valour of two hundeitht merkis; thre grite boittis, price fourty merkis*

The feather beds and other furnishings indicate a very comfortable level of accommodation at the castle, while so many pieces of artillery suggest that the Grants had anticipated some level of attack. The rigorous looting of Glenurquhart is perhaps best demonstrated by the fact that not only did the MacDonalds remove tables, beds, chairs and benches but also locks, doors and gates. The three great boats are a reminder of the use of Loch Ness in serving the castle. Before roads capable of taking wheeled traffic were built in the 18th century, any material of any weight, such as the pieces of artillery, are likely to have been brought by water and it would have been entirely sensible if these boats were also used to ship the booty back down towards Lochaber.

The inventory of stolen goods also gives us details of life in the Glen. Several trades are referred to, indicating that the economy of Glenurquhart was not simply a matter of subsistence farming. The inhabitants included a merchant at Balmacaan and another at Drumbuie, a clerk at Borlum, the sons of a forester at Culnakirk, and two shoemakers in Gartally and Drumbuie. Such tradesmen did not survive on their trade alone; the local tailor, a man called Ewen Bain, lived on the Borlum lands and, in addition to making clothes, he farmed his land with 19 cattle, a horse, 22 sheep and a dozen goats. Similarly, his neighbour, John Makmul, ran a small farmstead but was also identified with an occupation – bowman or cowherd. At Polmaily we find William McGowan and Baak, '*Gow Roy's daughter*'. The names of both these people are related to the Gaelic word *gobha*, meaning a blacksmith, and there are a variety of local legends of *An Gobha Mor* of Polmaily. Even if there is no family connection between William, Baak and the legendary big blacksmith who won an enchanted filly from the fairies, it would appear that Polmaily was the location of the main forge in Glenurquhart.

Most people mentioned in the list do not seem to have used a surname but, as was usual in the Highlands, their patronymic instead, such as William McPatrik McEane Vayne of Easter Inchbrine. For this reason it is not surprising to see only two men in Glenurquhart who use the name Grant. One of them is John Grant of Balmacaan who would appear to be the laird of Freuchie's heir. Although residing at Balmacaan, which would become the centre of estate business in the coming centuries, he does not appear to have kept animals himself other than eight horses, as befitting a gentleman. This pattern of ownership is repeated by Mr James Farquharson, the parish priest, who kept six horses. While it would appear that animal husbandry was not considered suitable for the higher levels of society, such was the economic importance of cattle that it is not surprising that the owner of by far the largest number of cattle was the laird of Grant himself, who lost 250 beasts to the MacDonald raiders.

Restitution and alliances

It might be expected that a raid of this scale might result in a punitive campaign organized with royal sanction. However, the Rough Wooing – England's attempt to win the hand of the infant Mary, Queen of Scots by force – and the rising of Donald Dubh in the west presented the Crown with bigger problems, and James Grant was left to find redress as best he could. Like his father after the raid of 1513, he turned to the courts rather than attempting any show of force himself. Legal summonses were pronounced at the market cross in Inverness, since it was felt that there would be no safe passage for legal officers to serve summonses at the homes of the offenders in Lochaber and Moidart. On 22 October 1546, the verdict was given that the offenders should return the stolen goods or pay compensation totalling £718 11s 1d to the laird of Glenmoriston, and the immense sum of £10,771 13s 4d to the laird of Freuchie. Two of the culprits, Ranald Mor MacDonald of Keppoch and Ewen Allanson, captain of Clan Cameron (and the father-in-law of the laird of Freuchie's sister, Agnes), lost their heads, partly in punishment for the great raid and partly because of their involvement in the rebellion of Donald Dubh.

While heads rolled, the compensation was not forthcoming, and in May 1547 the fine was commuted into the confiscation of estates. The MacDonald of Glengarry lands of Lochalsh, Lochcarron, Lochbroom, Morar and Glengarry itself, along with the Cameron lands of Lochalsh and Kishorn with Strome Castle, were granted to the lairds of Freuchie and Glenmoriston. However, they were just as powerless to enforce entry to their new lands as the courts had been in enforcing the payment of compensation. Instead, they used their legal claims to the lands as bargaining tools in bringing some semblance of harmony to the Great Glen.

In 1547, James Grant of Freuchie and John Mor Grant met their nephew, Ewen Beag Donaldson, the new captain of Clan Cameron, and agreed a pact whereby, in return for Clan Cameron's good behaviour, the Grants would not press their claim on the Cameron lands. The previous pact of goodwill in 1520 had been broken by the Clan Cameron and it is perhaps a reflection of the importance placed on such parchments by the Camerons that Ewen Beag required the assistance of James Farquharson, the priest of Glenurquhart, in order to sign his own name. The Grant claim to the MacDonald of Glengarry lands remained an issue until as late as 1600, although the marriage of Helen Grant, daughter of the John, fourth laird of Freuchie, in 1571 to Donald Mcangus Mcalestir of Glengarry may have been intended to carry with it the Glengarry lands as a dowry.

The fourth laird of Freuchie, John 'the Gentle', had nine children and used their marriages both to strengthen existing alliances and to attempt to heal wounds. His son Duncan married Margaret MacKintosh, daughter of the chief of the Clan Chattan, strengthening a bond with a clan whose political allegiances often varied. As well as marrying Helen into the Glengarry family, John Grant married other daughters into the families of the MacKenzies of Kintail, who were a rising power in the north-west, the Frasers of Struy in Strathglass, and the Gordons of Baldornie. During the rest of the 16th century, the Grants continued to consolidate their position through forming bonds with their neighbours rather than by attacking them. This even stretched to an alliance being forged between the John Grant, the fifth laird of Freuchie and Allan of the Red Shirt, the owner of the crannog on Loch Lundie in the Glengarry lands. In 1602 Allan had been behind the burning down of the church of Kilchrist, near Muir of Ord, while a band of MacKenzies were inside. Such actions won Allan few friends but John Grant saw this as an opportunity to bind down such a troublesome neighbour. Allan owned woodlands in Morar and Grant, using experience gained from the timber trade in Urquhart, took on the harvesting and sale of the timber, splitting the profits with Allan. The arrangement was not only profitable but also ensured that the Grant estates were not threatened by this local brigand.

64 The upper parts of the tower with its elaborate barizans and decorative corbels were added by John Grant, 6th laird of Freuchie in 1623

While the policy of creating a network of bonds among their neighbours in the Great Glen is a pattern of behaviour that characterizes the Grants in the late 16th century, it does not imply that the Grants were any more virtuous in their dealings than their neighbours. Iain Mór a' Chaisteal (Big John of the Castle) was the third laird of Glenmoriston. He was renowned for his strength and for his charismatic leadership, and he held the position of chamberlain of Urquhart, although he lived at Balmacaan. Iain Mór was given commissions to bring to an end disturbances among the Clanranald and the Clan Cameron and he appears to have been one of the most powerful men in the Glen in the first third of the 17th century. However, he also murdered a travelling merchant and avoided prosecution largely as a result of his usefulness to the government. In 1620, he gave shelter to members of the Clan Chattan who had just raided the lands of the earl of Moray. Although prosecuted for this, the case was allowed to drop following the personal intervention of Charles I, whom Iain Mór had travelled to London to impress.

Elaboration and industry

By the early 17th century, Balmacaan had become firmly established as the residence of the chamberlain of Urquhart. This post, generally held by a kinsman of the laird of Freuchie, often a younger son, was required to manage the Urquhart estate while the laird himself was normally resident on the main Grant estates in Strathspey. Urquhart Castle seems to have been reserved for the laird's occasional visits to Glenurquhart but it is likely to have suffered some neglect. In 1623, John Grant, the sixth laird of Freuchie, commissioned John Moray, master mason to '*wolt* [vault] *the hous heid of Urquhart*' (**64**). The fifth laird had died the year before and it would appear that the new works were the act of his heir setting out to make his mark on his new estates. The result of the work was the vault over the upper storey of the tower, with is square, roofed bartizans, the parapet wall carried on a double row of corbels and the machicolations over both the main door and the door to the basement on the east side of the building. The alterations had functional benefits in a period when defence was still an active issue: small rooms were provided in the bartizans with fireplaces for the accommodation of watchmen; the machicolations provided additional protection for the doors; and the flat roof could act as platform for artillery. However, the overall effect was more threatening than dangerous; the improvement in the defences of the building was slight but it was now equipped with the elaborate superstructure suitable for a fashionable residence.

As well as spending money on the refurbishment of his own residence Sir John Grant looked to find other ways to make his estates profitable. In 1634, he made over much of his Glenurquhart property, including the castle, to his wife, Marie Ogilvy, as her jointure, but specifically reserved his

> *liberty to draw dams and passages to the ironworks in Wrquhart, with liberty to put and build the said ironworks on the lands, providing Sir John and his foresaids upheld*

the rental of the lands wherethrough and whereon the said dams, passages, and ironworks should be drawn and built, and reserving in the same way the use of the whole woods thereof for the use of the ironworks.

The remains of this early ironworks may well be the bloomery site near Loch nam Bat in the hills on the north side of Glenurquhart. The venture relied on iron ore being brought to Glenurquhart for smelting using the plentiful supplies of charcoal made from the woods of the glen. However, it would appear that this venture was about as successful as Sir John's dismal attempt at about this same time to establish a copper mine somewhere in the vicinity of Kilmichael.

Urquhart as a jointure house

Sir John Grant of Mulben, the sixth laird of Freuchie, died in Edinburgh on 1 April 1637 and was buried at the chapel of Holyrood. Aged 39, his death was not anticipated and he drew up his will hurriedly from his deathbed. For the previous two years, his heir, James, had been following a military career, which included a spell overseas fighting for the Swedish army under Field Marshal Leslie (**65**). As the heir to the Grant estates, James now abandoned the army life at the age of 21 to take up his inheritance. The estate that he received was not a happy one, burdened with many debts, with much of the estates held in wadsets and with two dowagers, the new laird's mother, Marie Ogilvy, and grandmother, Lilias Murray, to support.

Being drafted in a hurry, the will does not appear to have been particularly well thought through. The joint executors of the sixth laird were his son James and his wife, Marie Ogilvy. Such an arrangement was common and was intended to ensure that the will served the interests of both the widow and the heir of the estate. It is possible that Sir John, on his deathbed, was aware that there were going to be problems between his wife and his eldest son and was making sure that neither of them could abuse their position as executor.

In the event Marie Ogilvy and the new laird found the situation unworkable, and Marie resigned her role as co-executrix because of '*the great troubill, trawellis and chargis*' that the role would bring and the '*great fascherie*' or disturbance that would occur if she tried to take her share of her husband's furnishings and other moveable goods. However, this resignation was not without strings, and in return for giving her son a free rein he granted her the lease until her death of the lands of Urquhart, which had been made part of her jointure in 1634, and several other properties in Strathspey. The benefits to the estate of this arrangement are likely to have been slight and the agreement appears to have been primarily aimed at avoiding arguments between a mother and son who do not appear to have seen eye to eye; as Marie took up residence in Urquhart Castle she was going to be many miles away from her son in the Grant heartlands of Strathspey.

Marie Ogilvy's residence at Urquhart Castle is the last occasion on which Urquhart acted as a lairdly residence. One consequence of the settlement that she had

65 *James Grant, 7th Laird of Freuchie*

reached with the seventh laird was that she now lived in Urquhart Castle and had a free hand to manage the estates of Urquhart and Corrimony as she saw fit, an echo of earlier days. She certainly emulated the role of the previous occupants of the castle in ensuring order within the bounds of the estate. Local stories relate that Culnakirk, above Milton, was occupied by a family of MacDougalls, known as the Dughallaich 'Ic Phadruig, who held their land from the laird of Glenmoriston. At a funeral for one of the Glenmoriston family at Kirkhill tensions between the MacDougalls and some of Lady Ogilvy's tenants spilled over into a vicious fight. Swearing vengeance, the MacDougalls later killed the miller of Wester Milton, one of the leaders of the opposing side, in his own house. This merely escalated tension and Lady Ogilvy intervened to resolve the matter and bring the murderers of her tenant to justice.

She ordered the arrest of Dugald mac Ruairi, the leader of the MacDougall gang, who evaded capture by hiding out in the surrounding woods. His wife, Mairi, refused to reveal where he was hiding; she was taken from their house and placed '*in the lowest vault of the castle*'. However, the days of the undisputed authority of the occupant of Urquhart Castle had passed, and Patrick Grant of Bealla-Do in Glenmoriston demanded the release of Dugald mac Ruari's wife or he would consign the castle to the flames. Marie Ogilvy ignored his threats and he, as a result, burnt down her farm buildings, probably at Strone or Borlum. Incensed, she ordered her tenants to exact punishment for this injury by carrying out a raid on the arsonists in Glenmoriston. However, they refused to do this, and Lady Ogilvy was left fuming impotently at the disintegration of her authority.

While it is tempting to see Marie Ogilvy's residence with her younger children in Urquhart Castle as a restitution of the status of the castle as the caput of the estates (the great stronghold with a noble occupant, having direct control over its lands), in truth she was an unpopular landlord who did not command the love and respect of her tenants. Indeed the disdain was mutual, as can be seen in a letter addressed to her son in 1646, where she said '*I allwayis knew the men of Urquhart to be knauis, and houpis er long to mak them sufer for it.*'

Covenanting and a divided family

While the animosity between Marie Ogilvy and her tenants fermented, there were other matters afoot that were to have a far greater impact on the Great Glen and, indeed, Britain as a whole. If Marie Ogilvy expected that her position alone should result in the unquestioning loyalty and love of her tenants, she was not the only one.

During the 1630s Charles I had been gradually implementing his ecclesiastical reforms. By 1638, however, resistance to his reforms crystallized in the National Covenant, drafted in February of that year. This manifesto set out an alternative structure for the Church, rejecting the episcopal reforms that Charles had been trying to bring in. By setting out this opposition in a reasoned form, a clear distinction was drawn between those who were in support of the king's policies and those who were not. The implications of this matter were felt well beyond the circles of those who concerned themselves with religious doctrine and practice, as it was an issue that also concerned those who feared for the distinctiveness of Scotland within Great Britain and those who resented Charles's increasingly autocratic style of government. The role of the National Covenant as a rallying point for dissatisfaction with Charles I's rule was emphasized when a copy was sent to each parish in Scotland. The members of the congregations were encouraged to sign it, and reports were prepared naming all those who had refused. James, seventh laird of Freuchie, signed the National Covenant within weeks of its drafting, and in the middle of March he was in Perth at a conference in its support. He was joined in his support of the Covenant by Patrick Grant; the fourth laird of Glenmoriston was active in trying to ensure that the Covenant was promoted throughout the Grant estates.

In Glenurquhart, however, the laird of Freuchie came up against two obstacles to his will. The Rev. Alexander Grant had been the vicar of the parish of Urquhart and Glenmoriston since the early 1620s, and had arranged for the decrepit churches at Kilmore in Glenurquhart and Clachan Cholumchille in Invermoriston to be rebuilt. He often failed to attend the Presbytery in Elgin and failed also, on occasion, to follow the proper procedures regarding the reading of wedding banns when it suited his parishioners. In short, he appears to have esteemed the interests of his parishioners above debates of the Kirk authorities. He had little sympathy for the views of the Covenanters and resisted signing the National Covenant. Almost the whole town of Inverness signed the Covenant in April 1638 and yet Rev. Grant remained faithful to the episcopal system. However, the pressures placed on him by the Presbytery and the two lairds of the parish, combined with the abolition of the episcopacy by the Glasgow General Assembly at the end of the year, resulted in his eventual, reluctant signing of the Covenant on 14 May 1639, in Forres.

If the laird of Freuchie's first obstacle to promoting the Covenant in Glenurquhart was Rev. Grant, the second, more formidable one was his own mother. Marie Ogilvy seems to have disagreed with her son on most things, and religion was no exception. She was devoted to the cause of the bishops and refused to see it undermined in her estates. In 1640 the relations between the king and the Covenanters had reached such a low pass that a Covenanter army was sent into England. The new military footing of the country required more fighting men and Major-General Munro toured the Highlands requiring the various landowners to send men to General Leslie and to raise taxes to support the fighting. With the stakes so high, Lady Ogilvy was obliged to agree to these demands, although her tenants did little to respond to them.

Montrose and the royalist army

Just as the events within the Great Glen rarely had much of an impact on the Lowlands of Scotland, equally there were only some events that took place in the Lowlands and beyond which had a direct impact on the Glen. Often the impact was one of the men of the Glen going off to fight, as when the men of Urquhart and Glenmoriston followed the earl of Huntly in his attempt to go to Mary, Queen of Scots' defence in 1567. However, over time the communications between the Highlands and Lowlands became swifter, and the Great Glen was caught in storms that raged across the entire country.

In 1643, the Solemn League and Covenant was drafted. This was a document which effectively superseded the National Covenant of 1638, and which was far more strident in its call for Presbyterianism to be established not just across Scotland but the whole of Britain. Only by accepting the terms of the Solemn League and Covenant did the Parliamentarians in England succeed in bringing the Scottish Covenanter army into the Civil War on their side. However, for some, including the seventh laird of Freuchie, it was too extreme a document and his dedication to the covenanting cause faltered. This reaction was shared by many including, most crucially, James Graham, fifth earl of Montrose, who abandoned the cause of the Covenant and, in 1644, was made a marquis and received the commission to lead the king's forces in Scotland.

The royalist cause faltered at first, but in July 1644 Alasdair MacColla, the son of MacDonald of Colonsay, landed at Knoydart with 1,500 men and marched up the Great Glen, before camping at Leitir nan Lùb between Loch Oich and Loch Ness and sending out the fiery cross to call men to the king's aid. Both the laird of Freuchie and the Tutor (or guardian) of the young laird of Glenmoriston made no response to MacColla's call; although their sympathies may have now lain with the royalist cause, it perhaps was still too reminiscent of so many other Clan Donald risings. Many of the MacDonalds of Glengarry and Clanranald, and the MacDonald tenants of Urquhart and Glenmoriston, were swifter in answering the call, swelling the numbers that went south with MacColla to meet up with Montrose.

Montrose and Alasdair MacColla's campaign across Scotland in the autumn and winter of 1644/45 is more fully related elsewhere. Their swift successes in Perthshire, Aberdeenshire and Argyll aroused an upwelling of support for the royalist cause and prompted the laird of Freuchie to quit his position of neutrality and send Montrose 300 men. While Montrose's skills as a military commander are rarely questioned, it is generally acknowledged that '*his successes were due as much to MacDonald's Celtic fire and knowledge of the Gael as to his own generalship*'.[3] This certainly appears to have been true of what is possibly the most remarkable feat of this campaign.

At the end of January 1645, having ravaged Argyll, Montrose was leading his men up the Great Glen towards Inverness in the hope of raising the clans in that area to join the king's cause. On 31 January Montrose and his men were camped at Leitir nan Lùb where, as he had hoped, he was joined by additional clans offering their support, including the Clan Cameron. However, he also received a messenger; Iain Lom, the bard of the MacDonalds of Keppoch, arrived with the news that the marquis of Argyll had landed with a force at Inverlochy, thereby presenting the possibility that the royalist army could be attacked from the rear if it encountered resistance as it advanced on Inverness. Montrose's response was to force a 65km- (40-mile-) march to confront Argyll. However, it was the local knowledge of men such as Iain Lom and the other MacDonalds of Keppoch that permitted his army to take Argyll's forces by surprise. Instead of heading straight down the Great Glen, he marched his men overnight up Glen Tarff, across into Glen Turret and down Glen Roy. Skirting the foot of Aonach Mór and Ben Nevis, his men arrived above the Covenanter troops at Inverlochy after dark on 1 February. Battle was joined at dawn on the following day, with the Highland charge causing a force twice as numerous to collapse. Montrose claimed that he only lost four men in the battle, against Argyll's 1,500 casualties.

By coming out in support of the royalist cause, the seventh laird made enemies of those who still adhered to the Covenant. His own house at Elchies in Strathspey was ransacked and at Christmas 1644, Urquhart Castle was attacked by Covenanters from Inverness, guided by the Tutor of Glenmoriston and assisted by disgruntled tenants on the Urquhart estates. The castle was looted and Marie Ogilvy was run out of the glen. The dowager lady of Freuchie lived with her daughter for another three years but she never returned to Urquhart. In 1646 she wrote to her son, hoping that those to whom he had entrusted the care of the castle would '*keep it well from these rogues*'. She was the last person to make Urquhart Castle her home, possibly establishing a garden beyond Durward's great ditch on the land running down to the shore of Urquhart bay. While Marie Ogilvy and the people of Glenurquhart appear to have held each other in mutual disdain, it would appear that the castle, at least, had a place in her affections.

Urquhart deserted

In 1647, James, seventh laird of Freuchie, ordered his agent to make an inventory of the contents of Urquhart Castle. With the death of his mother that year, he was able to assume the power of laird of Glenurquhart in addition to the title, and the inventory was an essential part of this transition. Since Marie Ogilvy's ejection from Urquhart, the castle had not been inhabited and the inventory is therefore of a deserted building. Indeed, it opens with the description of the '*mansioune and maner place of Wrwuhart being alluterlie spoilzieit, plunderit, and abvsed of the whole plenieshing, goodis and geir and insicht quhilk was thairintill and within the samene*'. The contents reveal a residence where all but the most basic furnishings had been removed, either by Marie Ogilvy as she fled or, more likely, by the Covenanters and locals once she had gone. A thorough inspection of all the buildings at Urquhart revealed that the entire castle except the tower had been emptied of anything movable. In the tower the remaining furniture was listed as:

> *in the chalmer above the hall* (first floor), *ane bed of tymber, and taffill* (small table), *ane furme* (bench); *in the wolt chalmer* (second floor), *ane bed of tymber, ane taffill; in the hall* (ground floor), *ane boorde* (dining table), *ane furme, ane taffill, ane chaire; in the seller ane old kist, without any kynd of vther wairis, plenishing, goodis or geir whatsumewer, in all or any of the saidis houssis and maner place forsaid, except allenarlie beare wallis.*

All this was estimated to be worth the paltry sum of £20. This inventory, however, was not intended merely as a stock take. By documenting the stripped state of Urquhart and getting the inventory witnessed by a public notary, the laird was seeking to ensure that creditors who had a claim on Marie Ogilvy's goods could not succeed in transferring that claim to him.

When James Grant inherited his estates from his father in 1637, they were burdened with debts, not helped by his father's profligacy and his failed ventures into iron smelting and copper mining. The care taken over cataloguing that his inheritance from his mother amounted to no more than a few sticks of furniture is in keeping with his general approach to his estates. Grant sought to ensure that the wadsetting of the estate was brought under control, redeeming these where possible or renewing them on more favourable terms. As was normal, he provided his brothers with homes on the estates. His brother Patrick had the farms of Clunemor and Clunebeg, while Thomas was given Balmacaan and, as was usual for the resident of this house, he performed the duties of chamberlain for the Urquhart estates. The laird's concern for finances led him to evict his brother Alexander formally from the estate of Mulben near Elgin for the non-payment of rent. However, despite his efforts, the turmoils of war and the taxation of the Cromwellian government left the estates as burdened with debt as when he inherited them, and it would be his son, Ludovick, who would restore the Grant fortunes later in the century.

¹ Register of the Great Seal of Scotland (translated from Latin).
² Mackay, W, *Urquhart and Glenmoriston: Olden Times in a Highland Parish*
³ Ibid., p. 153.

7

The relic

The army that Montrose led in the name of the King was, essentially, a Highland army. While the core of Alasdair McColla's forces may have been his Irish troops, he was a MacDonald and such associations counted. While the leaders of the neighbouring clans may have been reticent in allying themselves to what appeared to be an invading Irish army, a groundswell of opinion in Lochaber seems to have seen the royalist cause as an attack on the Campbell expansionism of the covenanting marquis of Argyll. This was one of the key factors that had brought the Lochaber clans into Montrose's camp. The role of Lochaber in supporting Montrose marked the area out as a bastion of pro-royalist, anti-Presbyterian support, which was tapped by the earl of Glencairn in his 1653 rising against the new Cromwellian occupation of Scotland. However, the clan leaders who came out for Glencairn were a new generation. Angus MacDonald of Glengarry, whose grandfather fell at Inverlochy, would remain a constant agitator for further royalist campaigns; Ewen Cameron of Lochiel, educated by his mother's family, the Campbells (but not sharing their views), was an intelligent and youthful leader who dominated Lochaber politics for the next 60 years. Keppoch was under the control of Alasdair Buidhe as Tutor of Keppoch, while his young nephews, Alasdair and Ranald, were safely abroad.

In contrast to the Lochaber clans, the Grants and Frasers were less supportive of the royalist cause, perhaps because they did not feel threatened by the covenanting Campbells. The Frasers remained covenanters while James Grant of Freuchie, as both a covenanter and subsequently a royalist, appears to have been something of a fellow traveller: Montrose had described the men Freuchie had sent to assist him as being '*bad and few*', at least that was before they deserted him. It is true that Freuchie raised 1,400 men for Charles II in 1651, but he delegated to his brother Patrick the honour of leading them at the disastrous Battle of Worcester. However, a distinction must often be drawn between the laird of Freuchie, with his estates around Strathspey, and the growing number of Grants in Urquhart and Glenmoriston who did not always follow the chief of what increasingly saw itself as a clan.

Despite the national, political turmoil, two particular aspects of the Great Glen remained; the claim of the Clan Chattan over the Cameron and Keppoch lands and the lawlessness of raiding. Neither was to be immune from the great changes that swept through the Glen over the coming decades.

Relations with Commonwealth and Protectorate

The recruiting success of Montrose in Lochaber appears to have influenced the decision of the ninth earl of Glencairn when, in September 1653, he called men to arms in the name of Charles II. The response by the MacDonalds of Keppoch and Glengarry and the Camerons under Ewen Cameron of Lochiel was a promising start, but the rising swiftly lost momentum. With few significant successes to galvanize support, Glencairn's men hardly left the Highlands. In January 1654, Ewen Cameron and lord Kenmure were sent to occupy the Grant estates both in Glenurquhart and Strathspey, and in March Glencairn was to be found passing through Urquhart and Strathglass with over a thousand men, probably en route to Dornoch to transfer command to John Middleton, a far more experienced soldier. However, the change in leadership proved fractious and by early summer the rising had dissolved. The Lochaber clans returned to their homes, fearing attack from the new English garrison at Inverness. At Glen Turret at the head of Glen Roy, the Camerons and the MacDonalds of Keppoch and Glengarry agreed to unite in the face of any English advance. In the event, the Cameron men were surprised by the English troops moving from Inverness to Inverlochy; Glengarry came to an accommodation with them; and the Keppoch men withdrew after Ewen Cameron berated them for the actions of their MacDonald cousins.

However, while the Glencairn Rising itself may have made little difference to the politics of the country, its aftermath was hard felt in the Glen Mór. Middleton became a hunted man as he sought, increasingly desperately, to find a route to leave Scotland to join the exiled Stuart court on the Continent. General Monck, the new Cromwellian Commander-in-Chief in Scotland, set off in pursuit and there followed a cat-and-mouse chase around the Highlands. In June, Middleton was reported to be in the Glengarry lands. Monck set off from Ruthven in Badenoch, burning Glen Roy on his way through to the Great Glen as part of a strategy that was both punitive and which denied Middleton support. Invergarry Castle was burnt as Monck then pursued Middleton through Glenmoriston into Kintail, which he also put to the torch (**66**). Rather than continuing the pursuit into the mountains of Kintail, Monck turned east across high country before meeting up with other English troops in Glen Strathfarrar and heading for Inverness via Glenurquhart. Middleton soon headed south into Badenoch, where he was defeated by English forces at Dalnaspidal, escaped to the hills and eventually found his way into exile.

By the end of 1654, the Glencairn Rising was an uncomfortable memory, and the Great Glen was, like the rest of Scotland, in the grip of the Cromwellian forces. The Lochaber clans continued to wage a sporadic guerrilla war against the occupying army but such resistance was slowly overcome by the new government's policies. By making local chiefs responsible for ensuring order in their own territories, the government reinforced rather than challenged the power of the chiefs in their localities. Furthermore, in an area where armed conflict was part of civilian life, the privilege of retaining arms was highly desirable but was only offered to those clans who cooperated with the new regime. Ewen Cameron of Lochiel, devoted royalist that he was, was also shrewd enough to see the benefit in marching his men to the ruins of Inverlochy Castle where, it was agreed, they would ceremoniously surrender their weapons before being granted the right to take them back for their own defence.

66 Invergarry Castle

This carrot was, however, accompanied by a very big stick. The Commonwealth's army was, essentially, a development of the English Parliament's New Model Army and operated along similar lines of discipline and systematic planning. It approached the challenge of controlling the Great Glen in a methodical and logical manner. The Commonwealth's navy had effective control of British waters, so Scotland was ringed with a series of citadels and forts, such as Leith and Ayr, which could be supplied by sea and act as military bases for operations on land.

Control of the Great Glen was to be achieved by a fairly simple strategy: new forts with clear lines of supply at either end of the Great Glen would enable a direct army presence in the area, and a ship on Loch Ness would provide direct access to the interior. Work on the first of the forts, on the south bank of the Ness between Inverness and the sea, started in 1652, when the following description appeared in the London paper:

> *The Major-General at his being here [Inverness] viewed a peece of ground, and gave order for erecting a large Sconce with five Bulwarks to hold about 2000 horse and foot; the wall is to bee of free stone, and will bee of great strength when finished, and very usefull and serviceable to the Commonwealth of England in securing for their use in these parts; the ground it is be built on is by an Arme of the Sea, and the river Nesse, over which there is a bridge to be made, and neare it there may ride ships of very great burthen, and in good harbourage. On Munday next they intend to begin with digging the grafts which are to partake of the water of Nesse.*
>
> *This day a Pinnace of above forty Tun was launched, which by the industry and exceeding paines of Captaine Pestle, Captaine of the Satisfaction, and some of his seamen, with almost all the officers and souldiers of Col. Fitches Regiment, was drawne*

six miles and upward over land, to the admiration of all that were spectators, it being a worke thought almost impossible. Considering the bulke of the vessel, and the ill way she was drawne over, I beleeve the like was never before undertaken; the men broke three cables seven inches about with hawling of her, yet it was incredible to see with what chearfulnesse she was carried away, though with great labour; there is appointed divers Souldiers and Seamen to bee put in her, and foure peeces of ordnance, and to saile up and down a standing water called Lough Nesse, which hath a property never to freeze, and is foure and twenty miles long, and in some places is two miles, and in others three miles broad, and lyeth betwixt the Highlands so that she will doe excellent service by preventing the Highlanders to make their passage that way, which is frequented by them.

Innernesse, June 14[1]

The Highlands had never seen anything like the new citadel at Inverness. This five-sided artillery fortress, encircled by a ditch large enough to take ships from the Moray Firth, was built following the latest theories of artillery fortification and was, to all intents and purposes, impregnable. The *Highland Galley*, which now patrolled Loch Ness, was a visible sign of Commonwealth presence even if it probably acted more as a moving watch-tower than a military force in its own right.

Two years later at Inverlochy, *'that ancient Castle … ruined by Times continued waste'*[2] was shunned in favour of a new fort with better access to the sea (**67**). Built with fewer resources than Inverness Citadel, it was, nevertheless, a bastioned artillery fortress that could withstand the attacks of the garrison's restive neighbours. The

67 *Inverlochy Fort as constructed by the Commonwealth army*

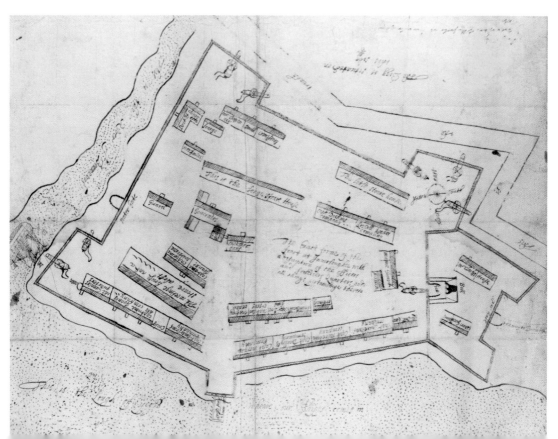

materials were brought by ship and it had to be built rapidly so that Ewen Cameron did not have time to muster an attack before it was defensible. Cameron's eventual reaction was to move house from Torcastle, 5km (3 miles) from Inverlochy, to a fine new timber house at Achnacarry, 15km (9 miles) away.

An order for equipment (although not necessarily fulfilled) gives some idea of the intended strength of the new fortress in the heart of Lochaber:

> *3 whole culverins*
> *6 demi-culverins*
> *3 sackers*
> *300 spear-pikes*
> *200 snaphance muskets*
> *200 collars of bandoleers*
> *40 felling axes with helves* (handles/shafts)
> *60 axes and hatchets*
> *A forge, anvil, vice, bellows, and other smith's tools*
> *2 sets of carpenter's tools*
> *1 ton of iron and 2 cwt of steel*
> *1 grindstone fitted*
> *1 double gin furnished*
> *5 barrels of pitch and 1 of tar*
> *1 pair of stillyards* (scales)
> *20,000 10d nails*
> *20,000 8d, 6d, and 4d nails*[3]

The armies of the Highland clans lacked artillery, which made any attack of a fortress of this strength suicidal. Instead, resistance seems to have been restricted to small-scale guerrilla attacks, which kept the army troops on their guard. The operations of which the army were capable were similarly limited to small sorties out from Inverlochy into the surrounding countryside.

As the Great Glen slowly came under Commonwealth control, General Monck grew more confident and considered elaborating on this simple arrangement of a pair of forts. In 1657, in a letter to Cromwell, he proposed:

> *a fort to bee built at the head of Loughnes, which will cost £7,000 (beside the charge of bedding). In it to bee two foote companies and 50 horse … So by the helpe of the forts at the head of Loughnes and Inverloughee it would bee a meanes to keepe the enemy from rendezvouzing at those places, which were heretofore the cheife places of their meeting.*[4]

Although Monck's fort at Kilchuimen was never built, it would appear that Monck was confident enough of his control in the north-west end of the Great Glen to propose using the *Highland Galley* as an alternative line of supply, seeing that the proposed fort would not have access to open water. It is also worth noting that Monck saw the isthmus between Loch Ness and Loch Oich as a meeting place of the clans; it was certainly where Alasdair MacColla chose to assemble his forces in 1644.

With the Great Glen held in a vice-like grip, it is not surprising that the Camerons were not the only Lochaber clan to enter into an understanding with the occupying forces. Angus MacDonald of Glengarry was more consistently hostile to the Cromwellian government than most, but even he could be found at Inverlochy beside Ewen Cameron, leading the local gentry in the celebrations of the accession of Richard Cromwell as Lord Protector in 1658. This rather uneasy acquiescence is associated with a transformation in the civil life of the Glen. For the first time in probably two and half centuries, the rule of law was supported by the exercise of force. It is not difficult to understand the reason for this change; '*the simple fact was that no previous government had ever looked so formidable, or behaved so reasonably from a position of strength in Glen More.*'[5] It was a harsh irony that a ruthless, military regime in London achieved the sort of peace and control over lawlessness in the Great Glen that had evaded the Scottish kings for generations. Restrictions on movement about the country kept raiders back from their quarry and the threat of attack no longer troubled the sleep of the people of Glenurquhart or the Laigh of Moray. The silence must have been deafening.

Restoration

The Restoration of the monarchy came suddenly in May 1660. Unlike the Commonwealth, it did not stem from many years of conflict but from the internal collapse of the administration under Richard Cromwell. However, it brought about no less a transformation of the country than the original revolution and invasion under Oliver Cromwell. Britain was gripped by an earnest desire to shake off the restrictions of the Protectorate's military rule. The regime's standing army was disbanded; the soldiers partly dismantled the forts at Inverlochy and Inverness and went home. In 1662, the laird of Freuchie was paid to finish the demolition of Inverness Citadel, an embarrassing reminder of the power of Cromwell. Suddenly both the constraints that had bound the chiefs of the Great Glen and the associated peace that the inhabitants had experienced were gone. Within months of the arrival of Charles II in England, Glenurquhart was once again the prey of cattle raiders from Glengarry. The 1650s may have liberated the inhabitants of the Great Glen from the fear of raiding, but it was a stifling liberty and appears to have been little mourned.

There is no record of Urquhart being used as a residence by any laird of Freuchie after Marie Ogilvy's death, and if it was occupied at all it is likely that it was simply for intermittent visits by the laird. Although the castle seems to have retained a role as the symbolic seat of the estates, Balmacaan, the home of the chamberlain, had taken on the functions of such a role. Indeed, a dispute in 1675 between Thomas Grant, chamberlain of Glenurquhart, and his brother, George, indicates that Borlum, originally attached to the castle as its home farm, was now part of the Balmacaan lands.

It was probably Thomas in his role as chamberlain who, in 1676, organized the last known repairs to the castle before its final abandonment. We know that the works cost 200 merks, or £133 Scots. A sum of this size is likely to represent substantial repairs rather than anything more ambitious. The works were primarily concerned with masonry, but the roof of whatever was being repaired was to be slated. The use of slate for a building of this date suggests that it was more than farm buildings that were being built but little else is known. It may simply represent essential repairs to the tower, the bartizans of which are likely to have been slated, which does not appear to have had any substantial maintenance for 50 years. However, the works could equally have involved the other buildings around the inner close, or the gatehouse.

The birth of Jacobitism

The reigns of Charles II and James VII saw little attempt to restrict the freedom of the Great Glen clans to destroy, steal and murder. The fact that the resistance in Scotland to James VII's accession was led by the earl of Argyll must simply have endeared this unlovable king to Argyll's adversaries in Lochaber. When James was eventually ousted in 1688, Lochaber once more rose in support of a deposed king. The leader of the Jacobite forces was to be John Graham of Claverhouse, viscount Dundee, who in April 1689, like Montrose and Glencairn before him, headed to the Highlands to recruit an army. His timing was fortuitous in that the MacDonalds of Keppoch were already mobilized in an attack on Inverness.

The year 1688, as well as witnessing the birth of Jacobitism, also saw the last great clan battle. The centuries-old dispute over the Lochaber lands owned by the Clan MacKintosh but occupied by the Camerons and the MacDonalds of Keppoch was reaching resolution. In 1665 the Camerons and MacKintoshes resolved their historic dispute, with Sir Ewen Cameron agreeing to pay 25,000 merks to Lauchlan MacKintosh for legal title to Loch Arkaig and Glen Loy. However, the MacKintosh claims to Brae Lochaber remained unresolved, and in August 1688, MacKintosh pressed his claim with a force that included government troops. Forewarned, the MacDonalds, with assistance from the Camerons and the MacDonells of Glengarry, attacked down the slope of Maol Ruadh defeating the MacKintoshes. The MacDonald victory at the 'Battle of Mulroy' brought instant retribution, with government troops overrunning Brae Lochaber and burning houses and crops.

When Dundee raised the standard of rebellion on 14 April 1689, Coll MacDonald of Keppoch with 900 men was extracting his revenge in the MacKintosh lands and terrorising Inverness for good measure. Keppoch's men were to become the core of the first Jacobite army. They were joined by Camerons, MacDonell of Glengarry, the Grants of Glenmoriston and the Grants of Shewglie – a rising family in Glenurquhart, holding several farms in wadset. Grant of Freuchie supported the position of the new government and the 1689 rising marks the start of a growing divergence in political sympathies between the Grants of Urquhart and the Grants of Speyside. However, it was not just the Grants who were split. While Dundee was assembling his troops in Lochaber, the Camerons raided Glenurquhart for supplies. They were confronted by, and subsequently killed, a MacDonald who lived in Glenurquhart and who had brandished his name as protection for his neighbours. The fact that a Cameron had knowingly killed a MacDonald almost split Dundee's forces in two, as MacDonell of Glengarry gave vent to his clan's indignation.

The death of Dundee at the Jacobite victory of Killiecrankie in July was the start of the end of the rising. With no replacement of Dundee's mettle to lead it, the rebellion rumbled on with the effective *coup de grâce* delivered on the Haughs of Cromdale at the beginning of May 1690. A settlement between the government and the Lochaber clans was agreed in 1691, and retribution followed. The punishment of the Grants of Glenmoriston was recorded by Lord Strathnaver, who commanded the troops sent out from Inverness:

> *I went out with a detachment from Inverness of five hundred foot, and three troops of Sir Thomas Livingston's dragoons, to Glenmoriston, where with great difficulty we forced open the iron gate [of Invermoriston House], not having a petard to blow it open. Some of the rebels very nearly escaped me, by a boy's acquainting them of our march. I burnt their corn, and drove their cattle and horses that fell in my way, to Inverness. This put them into such consternation that, notwithstanding our defeat at Killiecrankie, above fifteen hundred came and took the oath to King William and Queen Mary.*[6]

Final duty

Despite the harsh actions taken against Glenmoriston, the rebellious attacks continued for several months, and it was during this untidy conclusion to Dundee's rebellion that Urquhart saw its final military action. The castle seems to have escaped the attentions of the Cromwellian forces in the 1650s, probably because Glenurquhart, in comparison with the Lochaber end of the Great Glen, did not represent a threat to the new regime and because the building was empty. However, with Dundee's rebellion in 1689, men of Glenurquhart did rise and it is this that seems to have called the castle out of retirement for one last time.

From November 1689, the castle was garrisoned for the government by three companies of men under Captain James Grant. It was from here that an expedition was sent to Glenmoriston to apprehend Iain a'Chragain of Glenmoriston who, following the burning of Invermoriston House, had retreated to an improvised fort on Cragain Daraich near Bhlàraidh. The expedition succeeded only in injuring Iain's wife and daughter. However, in December, MacDonell of Glengarry, with 120 men, besieged the garrison in Urquhart Castle. The garrison maintained communication and supply with Inverness by water, using the medieval watergate and a leaking boat. Another 400 men joined Glengarry, largely drawn from Glenmoriston, the Chisholms and the Grants of Urquhart. By mid-December, however, Glengarry had to retreat to defend his own lands. It was a mark of how ingrained raiding had become in Highland life that Glengarry was not called upon to defend his lands from government attack but from Camerons, who were taking advantage of the absence of Glengarry men to steal their cattle.

The government garrison remained at Urquhart Castle for another two years and seems to have numbered somewhere in the region of 300 men. The accommodation must have been cramped within the tower, inner close and gatehouse. While the conditions troops were housed in were notoriously poor, they presumably supplemented the masonry buildings with tents and possibly timber buildings erected on the site of the ruins of the medieval hall and kitchens.

The oath of allegiance, which all clan chiefs had to take by 1 January 1692, had sealed the end of Dundee's rising. The last record of the garrison at Urquhart Castle is an order for supplies from Inverness on 11 January, and it is likely that the garrison was withdrawn soon after. This was the final military occupation of the ancient fortress: the departing troops made sure of this. In order that the walls should not shelter rebels as they had sheltered His Majesty's men, the gatehouse was destroyed with gunpowder, blasting vast masses of solid masonry to block the castle entrance (**68**).

The laird, Ludovick Grant, had raised a regiment who had fought for the government at the Haughs of Cromdale in 1690. In itself this had been a substantial outlay. However, with his estates subject to warfare his losses were far greater and he made a swift claim for compensation. At his insistence the commissioners of supply visited Glenurquhart, and in February 1691 reported that the losses sustained in the parish amounted to £44,333 5s 2d, and that this included a payment of £2,000 for '*damnifying of the house of Urquhart and low buildings by several soldiers of his Majestie's*

68 The gatehouse at Urquhart showing the masonry which blocked the gateway in 1692 when the castle was slighted

regular forces when they lay in Garison there.' In 1695, three years after the garrison left, the report was updated to add a further £30,000 to the bill for the loss of rent between 1689 and 1693. It is not clear why the slighting of the castle in 1692 does not appear to swell the bill in 1695. It may have simply been an oversight or, alternatively, Grant may have been aware that the enormous sums he was asking for were large enough already. In the event, although Parliament endorsed his claim, an ungrateful king never paid.

In 1708, 20,000lb of lead, which had been part of the lead roofing of the castle, were stolen from the vaults of the castle, along with 200 planks that had been part of the internal partitions. The lead would have easily covered 80m² (860ft²) of roof. While it is possible that the report of the losses was exaggerated, this would suggest that the tower, and possibly the gatehouse as well, had been roofed largely in lead. Ten years later, Alexander Grant was still pursuing the culprits from Buntait through the courts to get compensation. The fact that the lead had already been stripped from the roof and that Alexander Grant's complaint makes no mention of seeking repair of the castle makes it clear that by this point Urquhart Castle was derelict and redundant. The laird was objecting to the theft of building material, not damage to a house.

The final indignity came in 1715, when John MacKay of Achmonie reported that, '*The Castell of Urquhart is blowen down with the last storme of wind, the south-west syde thereoff to the laich woult.*' The stripping of the roof and, it has been suggested, explosive charges laid by the garrison in 1692, had left the great fortress so vulnerable it could be brought down by a gust of wind.

Fort William

The experience of Dundee's rebellion demonstrated that Inverness Castle with its lonely garrison was not sufficient to control the Highlands. In 1690, William of Orange, reacting to Lochaber's enthusiastic response to Dundee's call-to-arms, agreed to the rebuilding of the Cromwellian fort at Inverlochy, to be renamed Fort William in his honour. Its governor was to be Colonel John Hill, the same man who, 30 years before, had held Inverlochy under Cromwell; a man who had proved he could deal constructively with Sir Ewen Cameron and the other Lochaber chiefs. The dilapidated fort required major rebuilding. Work started on 5 July, and within 11 days, the troops had constructed a defensible circuit, albeit largely constructed of earth and timber. Permanent buildings took longer, and Hill had to negotiate the threat of desertion and mutiny among his 1,200 men for the first few months.

Other sites were also proposed for new garrisons about this time. Inverness Castle was the main garrison at the north-west end of the Glen, but the MacDonald houses of Invergarry and Keppoch were also proposed as sites by those particularly worried by the Clan Donald. Invergarry was commandeered for a garrison in 1691, along with other strongholds such as the old MacLean castle of Duart on Mull and the Clanranald seat of Tioram in Moidart. One further suggestion was taken forward: the establishment of a burgh adjacent to Fort William. Maryburgh, as it was known, remained simply the settlement of the camp followers for generations, but the idea that trade and development would bring peace and civility was a prescient one.

The reaction to the 1715 rising

In the Jacobite rebellion of 1715, the pattern of support across the Great Glen broadly echoed that of 1689, but there were differences. Sir Ewen Cameron, in his mid-eighties, had handed over the leadership of the clan to his heir, John. While John's younger brother, Allan, and many members of the clan joined the rising, John held back from committing the clan itself to the cause of James VII's son. The men of Urquhart and Glenmoriston again defied their chief by joining the rebels, to the fury of Colonel Alexander Grant, the eldest son of Ludovick, eighth laird of Freuchie, who had been given the Urquhart estates on his marriage in 1699.

Ludovick Grant was one of those men who stand out in a family history. Unlike his spendthrift grandfather John and his ineffectual father James, Ludovick managed to increase the wealth of his estates and gain favour through his solid support of the government. In 1694, his combined estates of Freuchie, Urquhart and others were built into the regality of Grant, with Ludovick assuming the new title of laird of Grant. In 1700, he was in a position to raise a Grant regiment for the government, funded for a year from his own pocket. It was not for nothing that this wealthy and influential man was nicknamed 'The Highland King'.

However, while the Grants were split in their loyalties during this period, it was the Frasers who were subject to the greatest somersaults in their fortunes. The coincidence of a disputed succession, the expansionism of the MacKenzies and the unpredictability of Simon Fraser, Lord Lovat, threw the estates of the Aird and Stratherrick into turmoil. Accused of rape and with the estates heavily in debt, Simon made his way to the exiled Jacobite court in France. While he was seeking favour there, the MacKenzies, through a strategic marriage and the calling in of debts, took over the Fraser estates and titles. While they managed to effect control of the Aird, stout resistance in Stratherrick continued throughout the first decade of the 18th century. Simon Fraser was devious, cunning, self-serving, manipulative and violent – qualities that were both the cause and the cure of his problems. A Jacobite rising in 1715 was foreseen, and Fraser turned coat again to return to Scotland to fight for George I, knowing that his adversaries, the MacKenzies, would join the Jacobites. His gamble paid off and with the victory of the government he was restored to the Fraser estates and titles.

Following the 1715 rebellion, MacDonell of Glengarry surrendered and was pardoned, but John Grant, Iain a'Chragain, the laird of Glenmoriston did not submit and suffered both the burning of Invermoriston House and the forfeiture of his estates. However, he had been canny enough to ensure that virtually the whole of Glenmoriston was held in wadset by different members of his family, including his wife, which greatly restricted the power of the Forfeited Estates Commissioners to seize his lands.

For those responsible for the government forces in the Great Glen, the 1715 rising had been an embarrassment. Fort William was in poor repair, with a depleted and unhealthy garrison. The isolated outposts of Tioram and Invergarry were swallowed up with little effort by the rebellious clans and the best that those stationed in Lochaber could do was send reports. The total failure of the existing military installations to control the Highlands made it clear that improvements had to be made, but there was little enthusiasm for grand gestures. The resulting reaction was visible enough to look like an effort but cheap enough not to hurt. Four new, lightly defended barracks were constructed across the Highlands: at Inversnaid on Loch Lomond, Ruthven in Badenoch, Bernera looking out to Skye and at Kilchuimen, finally answering Monck's call for a base at the head of Loch Ness. Kilchuimen, the largest of the four, seems to have been finished by the beginning of the 1720s and provided sufficient space for six companies, approximately 360 men, although it rarely, if ever, appears to have been filled. This programme of barrack building represented an attempt to reach a compromise between the two strategies of placing many small garrisons across the Highlands and spending large sums on impregnable artillery defences that were rarely likely to have to face artillery.

69 Field-Marshal George Wade by Johan van Diest. Wade is shown in front of his new road into the Great Glen over the Corrieyairack Pass

General Wade

In 1724 Simon Fraser, Lord Lovat, prepared a schedule of measures which he believed would help bring civil order to the Highlands and presented it to George I. Recounting the problems of cattle raiding, the associated blackmail and protection rackets, and the huge numbers of arms at large, he proposed a number of measures that could be taken to bring the Highlands into a healthier state, many of which involved giving certain men, such as Fraser, greater powers. The king's reaction was cautious and had far-reaching consequences. He sent a trusted Irish soldier, Field Marshal George Wade (**69**), to the Highlands to look into the problems reported by Fraser. Wade had proven himself both in battle and in the more subtle arts of Jacobite hunting and could be trusted to prepare an impartial report. Wade's assessment was ready by the end of the

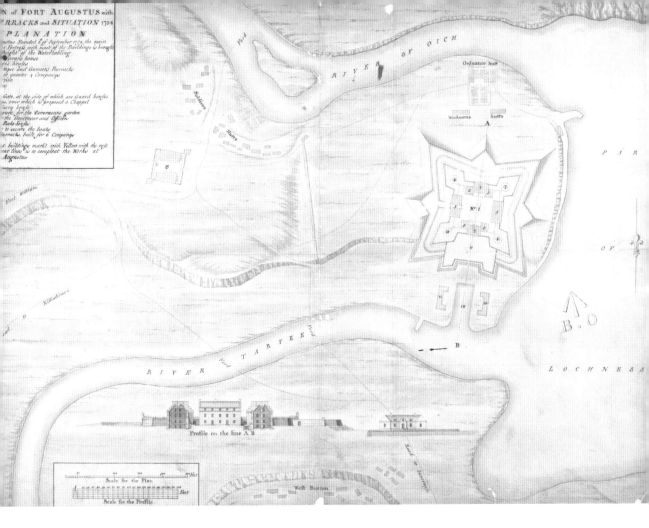

Profile on the line A B

Scale for the Plan.

Scale for the Profile.

year; he agreed that there was a pressing need for the effective disarmament of the Highlands, that over half the population could be induced to rise against the King and that the provision of forts and barracks was not sufficient to provide effective control. His proposals dealt with both operational matters and infrastructure; he proposed the establishment of independent companies of men intended to keep civil order and control raiding and, breaking with the policies of previous advisers, he suggested that the men of these companies should be able to speak Gaelic.

Inverness Castle was to be remodelled '*as well for preventing the Highlanders descending into the Low Country in time of Rebellion, as for the better Quartering of his Maty's Troops*'. Work started on Fort George, as Inverness Castle was now to be known, in 1727, incorporating the earlier tower as officers' accommodation within a larger complex defended by artillery bastions. Repairs were carried out to Fort William and, also in 1727, work started on a third, entirely new fort. Wade had not been content with Kilchuimen barracks, feeling that they were too small and should have been built with direct access to Loch Ness.

The new fort at Kilchuimen, built on the site of Thomas of Thirlestane's motte of Abertarff and replacing the barracks, was to be named Fort Augustus (**70**). Like

70 Drawing showing the proposals for Fort Augustus 1734

119

Cromwell's citadel at Inverness in the previous century, the opportunity of a fresh site produced a fort that followed the geometric principles of artillery fortification. Fort Augustus was to be a square fort with pronounced bastions, connected to a harbour built into the bank of the River Tarff where it flowed into Loch Ness. In the event the harbour was never built, with its role taken by a small pier that curved directly into the waters of the Loch. The fort itself was a set piece both of modern defences and of military architecture; a startling symbol of national government in Glen Mór.

However, Wade's great legacy to the Highlands was not destined to be these forts but the roads that connected them. In 1725, the road between Fort William and Kilchuimen was described as '*hardly possible for a single man*' and Wade himself complained that '*The Highlands of Scotland are still more impracticable, from the want of Roads and Bridges, and from excessive Rains that almost continually fall in those parts.*' One of the lessons of the 1715 rising was the vulnerability of isolated garrisons, which could be easily overrun before reinforcements could reach them. Communications across the Highlands were a priority for Wade. Improvements were partly achieved through the construction of a new *Highland Galley* on Loch Ness to supply Fort Augustus, but principally through the system of roads with which Wade's name is still associated. The first road Wade turned his attention to was the road through the Great Glen, which would link his three points of strength. In early 1728 Wade could report to George II:

> *That the great Road of Communication extending from the East to the West Sea, through the middle of the Highlands, has been successfully carried on upon the South side of the Lakes from Inverness to Fort William, being near 60 miles in length, and is made practicable for the March of Artillery or other Wheel Carriage, as may appear from my having travell'd to that Garrison the last Summer in a coach and Six Horses to the great Wonder of the Inhabitants, who, before this road was made, could not pass on Horse-back without Danger and Difficulty.*[7]

However, Wade was not simply creating a rapid way of getting from Inverness to Fort William. The forts and the road were part of a defensive structure that threw a cordon across the Highlands. Wade described the new Fort George's importance as being that '*it is built within half Musket Shot of the Bridge at Inverness and Consequently commands that pass which is the only communication between the North and South Highlands for the Space of near 30 English Miles as far as Killihinmen [Kilchuimen]*'.[8] In this connection it is interesting to note that, as Wade made clear, his road along Glen Mór stuck rigidly to the south side of the Glen. Wade seems to have been following the same principles of defence as those that had guided the construction of Hadrian's Wall and the Antonine Wall, the great Roman lines of control thrown across Britain: running from coast to coast with regular forts along their length connected by a military way (a term which Wade used to describe his roads). In terms of the Great Glen, a wall or ditch was not needed: Wade could rely on a string of lochs and rivers to provide the defensive barrier behind which his troops could move, safe from attack from the North.

1745 and the agents of change

Wade's vision for the Great Glen, a defensive line of control across the country, is of an impressive scale and remarkable clarity. The great irony of history is that it was a failure. The first shots of the 1745 rising took place at Wade's high bridge over the River Spean and his road only ever helped one army – the troops of Charles Edward Stuart, Bonnie Prince Charlie – as his forces picked up momentum in their sweep south (**71**). Fort George in Inverness, built on a bank of glacial gravel, was quickly undermined, and Fort Augustus fell when Jacobite mortars struck its magazine. Fort William held out resolutely and was a vital base for the government in the heart of Lochaber. When the rising collapsed after the defeat of the Jacobite forces at Culloden, east of Inverness, in April 1746, the presence of an active garrison at Fort William made the position of the rebellious Lochaber clans impossible. The government forces, under the Duke of Cumberland, were merciless and indiscriminating in the vicious retribution they inflicted on the Great Glen. Property was burnt or seized by the wave of government troops that streamed down Glen Mór. With the Jacobite forces hopelessly fractured, the best that Charles Edward Stuart's supporters could hope for was merciful terms of surrender or exile.

The romanticism that has surrounded the 1745 rising in support of that dashing, charming, self-seeking, false hope, Charles Edward Stuart, has affected the multitudinous interpretations of the behaviour of the clans. Sir James Grant of Grant tried to keep his clan out of the rising altogether; he supported the status quo, but was disillusioned with a government which he felt did not reward the efforts of a loyal supporter. However, the increasingly alarmed letters from John Grant, the factor at Urquhart, in the autumn of 1745 recount that many of the inhabitants of Glenurquhart were preparing to join the Jacobites. Many of the other clan leaders in Glen Mór seem to have had reservations about joining the rising but committed themselves in the full awareness of the high risks of this rebellion. The drama of the rising and the ferocity of the reprisals have overshadowed the fact that the changes which are associated with the defeat at Culloden were already in train long before Bonnie Prince Charlie set foot on Scottish soil.

The defeat of the 1745 rising was a political act, which had significant consequences. However, the changes that followed were not driven by the defeat at Culloden. With the failure of

71 Wade's High Bridge over the River Spean before the collapse of the arches

the Jacobites, the last conservative bulwark protecting the culture and traditions of the clan system was removed and the growing social and economic pressures suddenly found little resistance. Since the early 17th century, clan chiefs had been encouraged to restructure their estates away from an organization based on kin loyalty and paternal protection towards a more transparent structure based on leases and rents. Kinship ties are far stronger than those between a tenant and landowner, so such a reorganization suited the Crown and was resisted by the clans, particularly those in the West Highlands. However, inflation following the Act of Union in 1707 and the pressure on land of increasing populations all helped drive a desire to make the Highland estates more productive. This was behind the growth of the cattle trade through the 17th century, with its massive droves of cattle through the glens to markets in the south. It also lay behind the rise in rents, which, by the early 18th century, were pushing small farmers to the desperate point of emigration.

Since the early 17th century, the better-educated clan chiefs had seen stability and commerce as being a source of future wellbeing. By the early 18th century, the level of cattle raiding was lessening as the worst culprits moved away from violent theft towards the mercantile arts of extortion. Similarly, various attempts were made to diversify the economies of the Highland estates. Sir James Grant's failed ironworks above Glenurquhart in the 1630s was followed by the construction of an ironworks by Ewen Cameron of Lochiel at Achnacarry in 1678. This was a blast furnace that made use of charcoal produced on the Lochiel estates to smelt iron ore brought in from Cumbria. The furnace was destroyed in 1690 but a similar venture ran at Invergarry between 1727 and 1736. Each of these short-lived ventures represent an attempt by the inhabitants of the glen to make their estates profitable by using what they had plenty of, in this case wood to produce charcoal.

In 1756, the Board of Trustees for Improving Fisheries and Manufactures in Scotland founded a lint and woollen mill on the forfeited estates of Invermoriston. It was supplied with yarn by local women who were given spinning wheels for the purpose. The mill does not appear to have been a great success but it ran until 1791, when it was sold back to the Invermoriston estate and now forms the core of its home farm. Sir James Grant of Grant founded a similar but smaller venture in Glenurquhart at Kilmichael. Sir James Grant was a great 'improver', offering lime to his tenants free of charge in order to encourage them to adopt more modern practices of farming. In 1769, fresh from laying out his new planned town of Grantown on his Speyside estates, he turned his attention to Glenurquhart. His proposal was for a formally planned village to be called Lewis-town, in honour of his father Ludovick. He stipulated that:

> It should consist of one great street bout sixty feet wide & other smaller streets about twenty four or at most thirty as the moor is not of such extent as to admit of the greater Breadth – The lotts much likewise be much smaller than the Grantown lotts & square allowing no more for garden ground than absolutely necessary – the great street to be reserved for large houses & the present settlers all placed in the small streets.

The '*present settlers*' seem to have been tenants who had been moved off other parts of the estate by other improvements. The larger houses were to attract tradesmen who would invigorate the economy of the Glen. A new pier was built at Temple and a new road was constructed along the shore of Loch Ness to link Glenurquhart to Inverness. There had always been a track over the hills by Drumbuie and Abriachan but since the construction of the military road on the south side of Loch Ness, Glenurquhart had been effectively by-passed. The new road continued down to Glenmoriston but was not passable for carriages much beyond the new inn at Drumnadrochit. A publicly funded road running all the way to Fort Augustus and with new bridges at Drumnadrochit and Invermoriston was built in the opening years of the 19th century (**72**).

72 *The old bridge at Invermoriston, built by Thomas Telford as part of the new road between Inverness and Fort Augustus on the north side of Loch Ness*

Rehabilitation of the Highlands

In 1737 Edmund Burt had recorded the reactions which the new military roads across the Highlands elicited; the poorest people complained that roads were too hard for their feet, the '*middling order*' complained that the roads were too hard for their horses' hooves and '*those chiefs and other gentlemen complain that thereby an easy passage is opened into their country for strangers who, in time, by their suggestions of liberty, will destroy or weaken that attachment of their vassals which it is so necessary for them to support and preserve*'. The views Burt reported proved to be right. The opening up of the Highlands transformed the region from being one whose reputation for violent lawlessness kept outsiders away to a destination for the adventurous. The late 18th

century saw the British Empire expanding vigorously and, from an English or Lowland perspective, the Highlanders were grouped with 'Red Indians' and patronized in the same manner. Within a generation, the image of the Highlander was transformed from a fearsome criminal to a noble, if picturesque, native.

The radical shift in perceptions of the Highlands and Highlanders in the later half of the 18th century was not merely a product of greater peace, access and trade. A shift in aesthetic sensibilities was also working in favour of a new appreciation of the Highlands. In the 1730s Edmund Burt described the mountains of the Highlands as

73 Urquhart as depicted Thomas Pennant's A Tour in Scotland 1769. It shows the romantic view of ruins and scenery which brought the first tourists to the Highlands

having '*stupendous bulk, frightful irregularity, and horrid gloom, made yet more sombrous by the shades and faint reflections they communicate one to another*'. However, by end of the century, the minister of Urquhart and Glenmoriston was able to say of his parish that, '*both the glens of Urquhart and Glenmoriston exhibit to the traveller an uncommon and picturesque view of what is beautiful, grand and sublime in nature*'. The first adventurous tourists who arrived in the 18th century came seeking such rugged grandeur, and the shattered ruins of castles such as Urquhart found new admirers (**73**). When the same minister described Urquhart Castle as having '*a pleasant and romantic situation, commanding a most agreeable view of Lochness, almost from the one end of it at Fort Augustus to the other at Bona, and also of the lands woods and hills surrounding the loch on the south east and north*', he was appreciating the castle in the same way as millions of people have done since. The transformation of Urquhart from a derelict liability to a noble treasure echoes the similar transformation of the Highlands, and goes some way to explain the inseparability of the two.

[1] Firth, C H (ed.), *Scotland and the Commonwealth: Letters and Papers Relating to the Military Government of Scotland, From August 1651 to December 1653*, Scottish History Society, Edinburgh, 1895, pp.358-9.

[2] Ibid., p.362.

[3] Calendar of State Papers, Domestic Series, 1654, p. 317.

[4] Firth, C H (ed.), *Scotland and the Protectorate: Letters and Papers relating to the Military Government of Scotland, from January 1654 to June 1659*, Scottish History Society, Edinburgh, 1899, pp. 367-8.

[5] Lenman, B, *Jacobite Clans of the Great Glen*, p. 34.

[6] Mackay, W, *Urquhart and Glenmoriston: Olden Times in a Highland Parish*, pp. 204-6, 2nd edition, Inverness, 1914.

[7] Salmon, J B, *Wade in Scotland*, Moray Press, Edinburgh and London, 1938, pp. 114-15.

[8] Ibid., p. 116.

Further reading

Many online resources now give ready access to information on Scotland's history and archaeology. www.rcahms.gov.uk provides access to CANMORE, the National Monuments Record of Scotland's database online. The Archaeology Data Service www.ads.ac.uk makes the entire run of the Proceedings of the Society of Antiquaries available online.

Urquhart and vicinity

Alcock, L. *et al.*, "Reconnaissance excavations on Early Historic fortifications and other royal sites in Scotland 1974–1984", PSAS, pp. 255–79, vol. 116, 1986, pp. 119–147, vol. 117, 1987, pp. 189–226, vol. 119, 1989, pp. 95–149, vol. 120, 1990, pp. 215–87, vol. 122, 1992.

Banks, I., *Urquhart Castle*, GUARD Report 769.3, Glasgow University, 2000.

Batey, C. E., "A copper alloy pin from Urquhart Castle, Inverness-shire", *PSAS*, pp. 351–3, vol. 122, 1992.

Callander, J. G., "Fourteenth-century brooches and other ornaments in the National Museum of Antiquities of Scotland", *PSAS*, pp. 160–84, vol. 58, 1923–4.

Grant, A., "Notice of the opening of a sepulchral cairn at Balnalick, Glen Urquhart, Inverness-Shire; with notes on cupmarked stones in Glen Urquhart" *PSAS*, pp. 42–51, vol. 22, 1887–88.

Kirkdale Archaeology, *Urquhart Castle: Archaeological Watching Brief September 2000*, Archive Report, 9th October, 2000.

MacGregor, A, "Two antler crossbow nuts and some notes on the early development of the crossbow", *PSAS*, pp. 317–21, vol. 107, 1975–75.

Mackay, W., "Notice of two sculptured stones in Glen Urquhart", *PSAS*, pp. 358–60, vol. 20, 1885–86.

Mackay, W., *Urquhart and Glenmoriston: Olden Times in a Highland Parish*, 2nd edition, Inverness, 1914.

MacKell, A. C., *The Glenurquhart Story: A brief survey of the history of Urquhart*, Inverness Field Club, Inverness, 1982.

Moloney, C, *An Archaeological Evaluation of Land Adjacent to Urquhart Castle: Data Structure Report*, Headland Archaeology, 2nd November, 1997.

Samson, R, "Finds from Urquhart Castle in the National Museum, Edinburgh", *PSAS*, pp. 112 (1982), 465–76.

Simpson, W. D., "Glen Urquhart and its Castle: a study in environment" in Grimes, W. F. (ed.), *Aspects of Archaeology in Britain and Beyond: Essays presented to O. G. S. Crawford*, H. W. Edwards, London, 1951.

Simpson, W. D., "Urquhart Castle", *Transactions of the Gaelic Society of Inverness*, pp. 51–82, vol. 35, 1929–30.

Simpson, W. D., *Urquhart Castle or Caisteal na Stròine, Inverness-shire: Official Guide*, HMSO, 1938.

Simpson, W. D., *Urquhart Castle: Ministry of Public Building and Works Official Guidebook*, HMSO, 1964.

Smith, C., Hall, D., Cox, A. and Cerón-Carrasco, R. *Urquhart Castle: Report on the medieval finds assemblages*, SUAT, 25th November, 1999.
"Urquhart Castle, in the County of Inverness", *The Builder*, vol. XXX, London, 17th February, 1872.

Will, R., *Urquhart Castle Visitor Centre Excavation*, GUARD Report 769.2, Glasgow University, 1999.

Great Glen and Highlands

Anderson, J., "On the Site of MacBeth's Castle at Inverness", *Archaeologica Scotica*, pp. 234–44, vol. 3, 1831.

Blundell, Rev. O., "Further notes on the artificial islands in the Highland area", *PSAS*, pp. 257–302, vol. 47, 1912–13.

Burt, E., *Burt's Letters from the North of Scotland (Introduction by Withers, C. W. J.)*, Simmons, A. (ed.), Birlinn, Edinburgh 1998.

Cowan, E. J., "The Historical MacBeth" in Sellar, W. D. H., *Moray, Province and People*, Scottish Society for Northern Studies, Edinburgh, 1993.

Fraser, W., *The Chiefs of Grant*, Edinburgh, 1883.

Gray, M., *The Highland Economy 1750–1850*, Oliver and Boyd, Edinburgh and London, 1957.

Hopkins, P., *Glencoe and the End of the Highland War*, John Donald, Edinburgh 1998

Kermack, W. R., *The Scottish Highlands: A Short History (c.300–1746)*, W. & A. K. Johnston & G. W. Bacon Ltd., Edinburgh and London, 1957.

Lenman, B., *Jacobite Clans of the Great Glen 1650–1784*, Methuen, London, 1984.

MacDonald, D. J., *Clan Donald*, MacDonald, Loanhead, 1978.

MacDonald, N. H., *The Clan Ranald of Knoydart & Glengarry: A History of the MacDonalds or MacDonells of Glengarry*, Forrest Hepburn & McDonald, Edinburgh, 1995.

MacDonald, R. A., "Old and new in the far North: Ferchar Maccintsacairt and the early earls of Ross, c.1200–1274" in Boardman, S. & Ross, A. (eds.), *The Exercise of Power in Medieval Scotand, c.1200–1500*, Four Courts Press, Dublin, 2003.

MacKenzie, A., *History of the Camerons; with Genealogies of the Principal Families of that Name*, A. & W. MacKenzie, Inverness, 1884.

MacKenzie, A., *History of the Frasers of Lovat*, A. & W. MacKenzie, Inverness, 1896.

MacKenzie, W. C., *A Short History of the Scottish Highlands and Islands*, Alexander Gardner, Paisley, 1906.

MacKenzie, W. C., *The Highlands and Isles of Scotland: A Historical Survey*, Moray Press, Edinburgh and London, 1949.

Maclean of Dochgarroch, L. (ed.), *The Middle Ages in the Highlands*, Inverness Field Club, Inverness, 1981.

Miller, J., *Inverness*, Birlinn, Edinburgh, 2004.

Piggott, S., "Excavations in passage-graves and ring-cairns of the Clava group, 1952–3", *PSAS*, pp. 173–207, vol. 88, 1953–55.

Roberts, J. L., *Feuds, Forays and Rebellions: History of the Highland Clans 1475–1625*, Edinburgh University Press, Edinburgh, 1999.

Salmond, J. B., *Wade in Scotland*, Moray Press, Edinburgh and London, 1938.

Sinclair, Rev. A. Maclean, *The Clan Gillean*, Haszard and Moore, Charlottetown, 1899.

General

Barrell, A. D. M., *Medieval Scotland*, Cambridge University Press, Cambridge, 2000.

Barrow, G. W. S., *The Kingdom of the Scots: Government, Church and Society from the eleventh to the fourteenth century*. Edinburgh University Press, Edinburgh, 1973.

Brown, M., *The Wars of Scotland 1214–1371*, Edinburgh University Press, Edinburgh, 2004.

Cruden, S., *The Scottish Castle*, Nelson, Edinburgh, 1960.

Dodgshon, R. A., *Land and Society in Early Scotland*, Clarendon Press, Oxford, 1981. *Edinburgh History of Scotland*, 4 Vols. Mercat Press, Edinburgh, 1965–1975.

Foster, S. M., *Picts, Gaels and Scots*, B. T. Batsford, London, 2004.

Grant, A., "Thanes and Thanage" in Grant, Alexander and Stringer, Keith J. (eds.), *Medieval Scotland: Crown, Lordship and Community*, Edinburgh University Press, Edinburgh, 1993.

Hammond, M. H., "*Hostiarii Regis Scotiae*: the Durward family in the thirteenth century", in Boardman, S. & Ross, A. (eds.), *The Exercise of Power in Medieval Scotland, c.1200–1500*, Four Courts Press, Dublin, 2003.

Owen, D. D. R., *William the Lion: Kingship and Culture 1143–1214*, Tuckwell Press, East Linton, 1997.

Smout, T. C. (ed.), *People and Woods in Scotland: A History*, Edinburgh University Press, Edinburgh, 2003.

Tabraham, C. and Grove, D., *Fortress Scotland and the Jacobites*, B T Batsford, London, 1995.

Taylor, W., *The Military Roads in Scotland*, House of Lochar, Isle of Colonsay, 1996 (Revised Edition).

Young, A., *Robert the Bruce's Rivals: the Comyns, 1212–1314*, Tuckwell Press, East Linton, 1997.

Glossary

Barrow A mound constructed as a funerary monument. It differs from a cairn in that it may be constructed largely of earth. As with cairns the form of barrows varies across geography and through time.

Bartizan A corner turret projecting from the top of a building such as a tower.

Bloomery A simple furnace used for smelting metals before the invention of the blast furnace.

Cist A stone lined space, often found within a cairn, in which human remains were deposited.

Cairn A stone mound constructed as a funerary monument, particularly in the Bronze Age. There are several types, such as a Clava cairn, which vary depending on shape and whether they contain cists or chambers.

Clootie or rag well Certain wells and springs throughout Britain have been venerated as holy places. One form of veneration is to tie rags (or cloots) to nearby trees, perhaps representing a prayer.

Concentric castle A castle whose defences such as ditches or walls are arranged in layers, requiring an attack to overcome each line in turn.

Crannog A loch-dwelling constructed either on an artificial island or on timber stilts (or more often on a combination of the two). Crannogs provided security to the occupants and were often linked to the mainland by a causeway.

Cup-mark The most simple element in the patterns of cups and rings found carved onto rocks. They may date back to the time of the first farmers in Scotland.

Currach A small boat made of a light timber frame covered in hides.

Donjon The main tower or keep of an early castle. Often positioned on top of a motte, it provided high-status accommodation and acted as a secure retreat if other defences were breached.

Dun A small stone-built fortification common in the Iron Age, in particular in the western half of Scotland.

Feu A form of rent derived from feudal arrangements where payment in produce or money took the place of military service.

Garderobe A form of toilet where the waste fell down the outside of a building or a in a shaft within its outer wall to be collected and removed from the bottom.

Gatehouse A building formed around the main entrance to a castle. Often the gateway is flanked by a pair of circular, "drum" towers.

Great hall The largest covered space in a castle was the location for public events such as feasting or the dispensation of justice.

Justiciar A royal appointment responsible for exercising justice of behalf of the monarch. In Scotland there were two posts, north and south of the Forth, although on occasion they were held by the same person.

Liferent A form of lease where the tenant had security of tenure for their own lifetime.

Motte and bailey This form of castle consisted of a large earthen mound, the motte, which sat within a larger defended enclosure, the bailey.

Machicolations The holes between the corbels which carry battlements projecting from the top of a tower or wall. Rocks or hot liquids could be dropped through the holes to strike attackers below.

Palisade A defensive wall made up of large timber uprights driven into the ground with no space between them.

Quern A pair of stones used for grinding flour by hand.

Roundhouse Large circular house, constructed mainly of timber, popular in late prehistory. Their remains are often visible as hut circles.

Shell keep A variant on a keep where a motte is crowned not by a single tower but by a stone enclosure within which are several structures.

Spine wall A wall which runs along the centre-line of a building, parallel with the building's longer side.

Square barrow cemetery Groups of square barrows are a distinctive survival of Pictish burial practice

Symbol Stone A stone bearing a carved or incised symbol. The term is usually reserved in Scotland for the stones carved by the Picts.

Watergate A gate leading from a castle to the sea, a river or a loch. Watergates were generally difficult to approach on foot and were therefore difficult to attack.

Index